Reversing the Slobification of America

Tips & Tools for
Effective Communication
Professional Behaviors
Thriving Relationships
...In Life & Business

by Debbie Lundberg

Copyright 2011 by Debbie Lundberg

Debbie Lundberg, inc.

PO Box 13248 Tampa, FL 33681

ISBN: 978-0-578-09650-6

Fifth Edition.

This material has been written and published solely for educational purposes. The author shall have neither liability nor responsibility to any person or entity with respect to any loss, damage or injury caused or alleged to be caused directly or indirectly by the information contained in this book.

Edited by LM Sawyer.

Book cover design by Sue Nance.

Reversing the Slobification of America

Tips & Tools for
Effective Communication
Professional Behaviors
Thriving Relationships
...In Life & Business

by Debbie Lundberg

With special thanks to my wonderfully supportive and fun husband, Michael Lundberg, and to my much-appreciated clients for all your ideas, insights, enthusiasm, feedback, keen eyes, and questioning abilities...as demonstrated in your contributions, direct or indirect, in this, *your* compilation book!

Contents

Introduction

Slobification Quiz

Section 1: Effective Communication

Contents Continued
Section 2: Professional Behaviors

Contents Continued

Section 3 - Thriving Relationships

Closing Comments

Introduction

"Be kind, for everyone you meet
is fighting a harder battle." ~
Plato

Congratulations and welcome to a collection of tips and tools for living and learning in an effort to be part of "Reversing the Slobification of America"™! Interesting enough, when people ask me "What do you do?" (which, by the way, is not the best first or second question to ask most people after you meet them), and I reply with "Author, speaker and coach on 'Reversing the Slobification of America'™", many people look down at their attire and share something like "I don't usually dress like this" or "Yes, people dress crazy now, don't they?". Sure, each of those statements may be true, Slobification is about communication, behaviors and relationships, and while dress can impact those, clothing and style/fashion, are not the focus of this book. Instead, this publication begins with a Slobification quiz and is presented in three complementary sections on the following: *Effective Communication, Professional Behaviors,* and *Thriving Relationships.*

Throughout the chapters within each of the sections, you will find a quotation for reflection, followed by specific coaching tips for your being the best you at all things you choose to do. Additionally, "LUNDBERGisms", or expressions I use regularly (in boxes at the close of chapters), along with Slobification Snippets (denoted as (*<Slobification Snippet>*), are sprinkled throughout for quick reminders and points of humor and reflection.

The push for providing this book began as an itch, almost an irritation, when I started realizing years ago that things that I thought were "common sense" (an expression I no longer use) and common courtesies were at best sensible and, at worse, surely not common. I began noticing people of all ages ignoring chances to show appreciation and demonstrate respect…and then seeing those same individuals readily complaining that they got no appreciation or respect. I came to embrace the idea that you get what you give…and I am fortunate, for I have been given a lot of unique, interesting, and even tricky situations for which my nerves, composure, and surely, my manners, etiquette, and courtesy have all been tested.

Through it all, there has been a blatant uncovering and belief I hold that very few people awake in the morning wondering how they can make someone's day miserable, their family life less-than-desirable, or their company fail, rather, there are a lot of people who have not been made aware or been afforded the surroundings, upbringing, or expectations, to express things kindly, respectfully, with thought and intent. So, after a few books and seemingly countless speaking engagements regarding it, I trademarked the expression "Reversing the Slobification of America". The thrust of the expression, and therefore, the actions suggested, are about effective communication, professional behaviors, and thriving relationships. Because the American collective IQ is not increasing at the rate of other countries, and I continue to see self-serving people slobify our environment, businesses, families, and culture, it is at a point where if we are not part of the solution, then we are part of the problem…and *Slobification is a problem!*

As you are selling your services and/or your products, I encourage you to know that you are more than what you do for a living, that you are not here for a long time, you are here for a good time, and that in our worlds, each of us has a choice: to go with the flow, or make the flow. Choose wisely.

You may be thinking "Okay, so you get to work with people on effective communication, professional behaviors, and thriving relationships...so what?" The ultimate results are the "so what"...what can you do with what I have observed, experienced, and/or coached around regarding these integral parts of our lives: communication, behaviors, and relationships.

As far as Effective Communication, please think about what you say, how you say it, and how it impacts people. Be present and want information. Remember knowledge isn't power, rather it is your application of knowledge that is powerful for you. Throughout the book, it will be suggested that you offer inquiries and ask questions. Ensure you listen.

Regarding Professional Behaviors, have integrity, earn trust, respect time, and believe that very few people aspire to make things worse, but rather long to be part of the betterment of situations in school, life, and work. Know your core competencies for your company and each person. Know your brand and your two-to-four areas of expertise. Learn them, promote them, own them, and do not divert from the path...even when it is "easier" to follow someone else's path.

And, when it comes to Thriving Relationships, value people over products, work to support your team over your bottom line. This is a performance test, not an endurance test, though, so thrive with life, learning, and giving back. Things don't get - done for only four reasons, and people are driven/motivated by only four drivers. I'll share ways to identify and/or address each of those shortly. In the meantime, keep in mind that people, and this includes you, cannot give 110% - it isn't physically possible – get over it, and get realistic about 100%! See each person for their value…meet them where they are and lead them where they are willing and able to go…and yes, sometimes that is outside your friendship, your school, your team, or even your organization.

Keeping that in mind, there is a silver lining of sorts! I tell people I may be the only life coach with a guarantee, and my guarantee is this:

If you read this book, and make no changes as a result of the tips and tools, absolutely nothing will change as a result of having read this book

….100% guaranteed.

The changes are up to you. So, I ask you: *What are you willing to do to be who you want to be and have the business results you want to have? How will you be a part of "Reversing the Slobification of America"*TM*?*

12

Through my experiences on both sides of Slobification, it's been realized there are only four reasons things do not happen in school, life and/or business. And, there are only four key drivers that motivate people to take a stand, take action, and take responsibility. If you get nothing out of this book other than these two things (yes, you can get more!), minimally incorporate and appreciate these two concepts of *Four Reasons* and *Four Drivers.*

Four Reasons

Remember, people make things happen...or not happen, so, if something has not happened, there are only four things/reasons contributing:

1. Someone did not know,

2. Someone did not know how,

3. Someone did not have capacity, and/or

4. Someone did not want to do it.

And, to remedy these situations/occurrences, you address them very differently, so if:

1. Someone did not know, *provide information*, and if

2. Someone did not know how, *provide training or coaching*, and if

3. Someone did not have capacity, *assess their ability fairly*, and if

4. Someone did not want to, *provide an attitude check* (often chick on *yours* first).

Attempting to analyze and interpret things outside these four reasons will be futile and frustrating...the challenge is to offer the appropriate solution based on the situation, and not just continue to provide one of the three regardless of the occurrence.

Whether it is your child doing his chores, or your team completing projects, ask yourself (and them, too) what one of the three things to address, and then provide the feedback and support to enable and encourage their success!

Four Drivers

Since people make or break things, they too are the ones with whom we seek a connection. People are driven, and therefore, motivated differently.

I charge you to embrace the idea that you will not motivate another person, rather you can inspire him or her. People are motivated personally, and inspired fairly universally. The beauty of tying motivation and inspiration is knowing *how to connect the two*. In order to even attempt that, you will want to know first, what drives each person. Fortunately for each of us, we are only driven by four things:

1. Time (how is it spent)

2. Money (make more, spend less)

3. People (who & with whom)

4. Opportunity (pride, title, travel)

Each of these motivators ranks in a different priority throughout our lives, and each of them impacts quality...quality of life, work, memories, etc.

As an individual, it will serve you well to consider the priority of each of these drivers for you. As a parent, partner, leader or colleague, it will be important for you to want to know other's drivers and priorities as well. It is through knowing whether time or money is of the essence that you will know how to properly incent (provide inspiration) to each team member to tap in (connect) with his or her motivation.

With Four Reasons and Four Drivers firmly in your mind, you are positioned to be part of "Reversing the Slobification of America" ™ . You are interested, making an effort, and ready to act! So, take the quiz, read the tips, and please remember most tips and my coaching in this book were the result of my doing something erroneously and learning from it…I hope some of these ideas, and your application of the knowledge, keep you from being in the same awkward spots I have been!

LUNDBERGism

The enemy of talent is dishonesty, the enemy of leadership is pessimism, and the enemy of commitment is apathy. Stick with your Talent, Leadership, and Commitment...it is the combination to win over dishonesty, pessimism, and apathy every time!

Slobification Quiz

"Men are respectable only as they respect." ~ Ralph Waldo Emerson

Reversing the Slobification of America

Are you Slobified? Now that you know about Slobification and, more intentionally and importantly, "Reversing the Slobification of America"™, are you wondering if you might be Slobified or how Slobified you may be? Rest assured, we are all Slobified, myself included, it's a matter of the degree we allow the Slobification to take over and remain in our lives. So, to get started, take the Presenting Powerfully by Debbie Lundberg Slobification Quiz below:

Please read the following statements and answer honestly. Your response options, and subsequent points are:

Not Even Once – 0 Points

Rarely – 1/2 Point

Sometimes – 1 Point

A Lot – 1 ½ Points

Quite Regularly – 2 Points

1. I wander aimlessly in a location expecting others to clear the way and anticipate my next move.
2. I place orders for food or process transactions at a bank or store while on the phone.
3. I turn away from people to do something else and say "I am listening to you" so that person knows s/he can continue speaking while I work.
4. I have answered or placed a phone call while in a checkout at a store.
5. I run late.
6. I have answered a call or text on a first date, at a dinner party or interview.
7. I readily email people who sit less than 100 yards from me.
8. I call people at work who are on the same floor as I am.
9. I ask people "how are you?" when I don't really listen (or care).
10. I RSVP yes to events and don't show and/or RSVP "maybe" to invitations.
11. I whistle, hum or sing to myself in public.

12. I have texted someone within the same room.

13. I chew gum while talking to others and/or presenting.

14. I wear sneakers to weddings, dinner parties, and/or funerals.

15. I have texted someone while at dinner with someone else.

16. I say "I am so busy", "I am too busy" or "I don't have time for that".

17. I ask people at work to "do me a favor".

18. I say "to tell the truth", "truthfully" "to be honest with you", or "honestly".

19. I walk into meetings late and disrupt them again by saying "sorry I am late".

20. I put my nametag on my left side, belt, waistline, sleeve or breast at events.

21. I have answered or initiated a call, email or text while in the bathroom.

22. I expect supreme service regardless of how I act.

23. I think blinkers on vehicles are optional for use at times.

24. I ask clients and/or customers "how may I help you?".

25. I wear lounge ware or pajama-type bottoms when I am out in public.

26. I litter.

27. I complain openly and freely even when my opinion is not solicited.

28. I send emails without subject lines.

29. I reply to old email subject lines with new information/topics without changing the subject line.

30. I have had my mobile phone ring (with sound) while in a meeting.

31. I have had my mobile phone ring (with sound) while in a movie.

32. I have had my mobile phone ring (with sound) while in a formal Presentation.

33. I park my car across more than one space in lots or garages.

34. I talk on my phone via Bluetooth or speaker.

35. I have worn a headset, earbuds or a Bluetooth during a wedding, funeral, interview, dinner party, meeting, or first date.

36. I announce when I have to go to the bathroom rather than simply excusing myself.

37. I call people after the proposed start of our meeting time to say "I'm running late".

38. I talk on my phone, text or surf the web during movies, plays/shows.

39. I call people hoping to get their voicemail so I don't have to talk to them.
40. I am guilty of not cleaning up after my child, pet or myself in a public place.
41. I act like I have a call and put my phone to my head when I see someone coming with whom I do not want to converse.
42. I say "no problem" instead of "you're welcome".
43. I say "have a nice day" or "there you go" instead of "thank you".
44. I let the door shut after me when I am in a hurry, even when I know someone is approaching the door behind me.
45. I do not give the courtesy wave after someone lets me in when I am attempting to merge or turn in traffic.
46. I say "sorry" for getting in people's way or wanting to get past them.
47. I tell people "I'll try" to do something they ask.
48. I opt not to use the expression "excuse me".
49. I write emails or texts to people when I am on the phone with someone else.
50. I wear clothes that do not fit me properly.

Total Points = Your Percentage Slobified

<35% - Not *too* Slobified

36-60% - Seriously succumbing to Slobification

>60% - Sound the alarms - you are Slobified!

You choose: are you good with being Slobified, or do you want to be part of 'Reversing the Slobification of America'™? The following chapters are full of ways to personally reverse your Slobification through effective communication, professional behaviors, and thriving relationships. The idea is not to overhaul you, rather to enhance your life and allow you to share, lead, and connect in new and intentional ways…and revel in the slight changes, outcomes, results, and successes you deserve from applying your new tips and tools.

Section 1:
Effective Communication

"The single biggest problem in communication is the illusion that it has taken place." ~ George Bernard Shaw

There is much noise in our society, with a lot of people talking, ranting, uttering, and expecting, and yet there is not an abundance of effective communication. Communication is not just words, or the lack of them. Communication includes perspective, listening, pacing, and much more. To be effective in communication, there must exist humility, pride, ability, and interest…with a drive to exchange and share with an openness and a firmness that leadership begets. These tips are specific and implantable to fairly immediately deem their value and experience your results.

Chapter 1
How and When Did Our Language Become so Dilapidated?

"Correction does much, but encouragement does more." ~ Johann Wolfgang von Goethe

Word choice is key. Messaging is important. Conveying a thought with sincerity is riveting. Because of this, it is nearly impossible to believe that in an average eight-stop day, one will hear thank you once and you're welcome .25 times. Yes, based on my own personal experience (and I am pretty consistently a smiling, grateful, positive customer), those are the statistics.

Is it that I am being ignored? Not necessarily, rather language and communication have sadly been minimized in many cases to "there you go" or "have a nice day" at the close of a transaction and no response or a nearly lifeless "no problem" or "no worries" when a person thanks another.

It will serve us all well to consider what we are implying when we chose to direct someone with "have a nice day" or "here you go" after such person has engaged in a service or the purchase of a product. The person who says those things has subtly, or after reading this you may think 'not-so-subtly', decided that his or her idea is more important than appreciation. I haven't yet met a person who expressed an interest in being told something to do/take over a simple thank you. Based on that, whether you work in the food service industry, provide hand crafted items, speak to inspire/train others, or are the CEO, do take the time to smile and show respectful appreciation with a "thank you". In the vein of efficiency (if nothing else), it actually takes less time to say "thank you" than it even does to muster "here you go" or "have a nice day". Please do not misinterpret my suggestion as being opposed to nice days, rather this is a recognition of the ability you have to thank someone and how much more value it offers about the transaction and/or experience than something to come in the future (their day).

Similarly, many of us have minimized what does follow as a response to a "thank you" or "thanks" from "you're welcome" to a nod, nothing or very commonly, "no problem". While I am not clear on where or how it came to be that the concept of thanking someone indicated there was ever a problem came to be, responding with "no problem" implies without stating that there is, or may have been, a problem. The same holds true for "no worries", so please resist the temptation to fall back on that tired expression, too.

<Slobification Snippet>
Now, let's please journey back to the 1980's...all of this was first on my radar screen when working at a fast food restaurant in high school...I would ask to please take someone's order, and the reply would be a blank look up at the menu followed by "I need..." You need? I remember thinking, believe

22

me, nobody needs this stuff. Having two all beef patties was surely no need. And yet, so went the please.

There is no rhyme or reason to using "need" for a request. There is not more ease in uttering the words "I need" over "please". It is just pure self-focus, thoughtless disregard for the other person, and an abandonment of manners…assuming someone was taught manners at some point.

Whether or not you were raised with "please" and "thank you" is irrelevant. At this point, you know about them. Please use them!

Not that I do not occasionally go to a fast food place or two, but more often than not, it is at a more formal seated dining establishment where I go out for meals, and observe that when a waiter or waitress arrives at tables (especially around The United States) to take orders, he/she gets "I need…". Now, when was the last time someone needed a chardonnay or a margarita, really? And, it is not just in food services where the blatant lack of awareness is prevalent…it is on the phone, in retail establishments, when planning weddings and even funerals. Yes, it is nearly epidemic that our over stimulated, bloated society is in need of so much when a simple please is not only proper and considerate, but something that will condition others to respond in kind. Please is not something added for impact when you really, really want something. That behavior is reserved (and not condoned) for four-year-olds, and the likelihood you are reading this at four years of age is slight. So, knowing this, when did "I need" replace

"Please"? The exact downfall of that courtesy has not been pinpointed, but the day it can be reversed is today!

Likewise, when you are in someone's way or want to get around or through, please do not use "I'm sorry" rather ask or state "Excuse me", as there is no need to be sorry for wanting to get around or through. I see or hear people at restaurants, in offices, at coffee shops, etc. and there is a lot of "I'm sorry"s and few "Excuse me"s. Using "Excuse me" will not diminish the meaning of a heartfelt, sincere apology when it is appropriate. When you want to get past or in a place where another is, embrace "Excuse me" and resist "I'm sorry", so that the other person comprehends what is happening and you are respectful to yourself and the other person.

When you do realize you overlooked someone/something or said something inappropriate, ill-timed, or just incorrectly, rather than reacting simply with "I'm sorry" replace that by responding with asking "Please forgive me for...". The reason for doing this is to make you vulnerable, relinquish control, and allow the other person to decide how he/she wants to respond. Asking "Please forgive me" means you know it is required/requested, and the person who was wronged is in a position to acknowledge and respond. You can then share "I'm sorry". Just remember, "I'm sorry" first means you are focused on wanting to feel better for you rather than letting the other person's feelings come first.

Using "please" and "excuse me", and even "please forgive me" appropriately shows self-respect and respect for others. Being respectful provides for an environment of courtesy and consideration...and who wouldn't want to be in that environment?

Another environmental or cultural oddity that continues to amaze me is the considerable number of people who believe they are offering an adequate opinion or response about their action or ownership, when they share an answer of "maybe" or "I'll try" or "I'm trying".

Maybe means neither yes nor no, and therefore, provides nothing further in the conversation or plans. "I'll try" is stating something like "we'll see". In other words, when someone states he/she will try to get something done or manage to accomplish a task, it is both alright and acceptable for it to happen or not to happen...as long as one bit of effort is put forth.

Such answers are what I call "pre-cusing" (pronounced like excusing with "pre" replacing the "ex".) This is a word I have created for people wanting an out or excuse after the fact. After all, if they have not fully committed, then they have an excuse if something does not come to fruition. "Maybe" RSVPs and "I'll try" when something is requested are both wimpy and irresponsible and are not to be offered...or accepted as replies.

When someone is looking for a response or reply, remember, your professional options are five-fold. *Professional* is the key here. It is not professional to state "maybe" or "possibly" as a firm reply, because it is not firm, it is not a reliable reply.

Your five professional options are:

1. No (No, thank you)
2. No with information
3. Yes with a condition or boundary
5. Yes with exception
6. Yes (Yes, please)

How so? Well, ignoring a request or giving a vague reply may buy time or get you off the hook for a bit, so to speak, but the two clear replies are yes and no. Within these responses, please remember that a no answer requires nothing else...no explanation or excuse. I recommend a "no, thank you", and I will leave that up to you. If you have a desire to share a particular reason to inform, not to rationalize or excuse, you may want to include that with a no per XYZ policy or no due to the fact that...

Yes, though, is a bit trickier. People say yes for many reasons, and I encourage you to know the reasoning behind your yes and express that. If you are full on board, give an eager "yes", even a "yes, please" if you like. When, though, you are stating yes with parameters, include the parameters. I call this yes with exception or boundary. A yes with exception or boundary is giving a time frame or a monetary limit, etc. A yes with exception is different, meaning you would normally not be in agreement or replying yes, but this instance is an exception...it is unique for some reason. Again, provide the reason for clarity in order not to have miscommunication or misinterpretation in future interactions.

As an example, if someone wanted to use a space of yours on a Saturday for a planning meeting the optional replies are as follows:

1. If you do not allow after-hours or weekend work in your office, the reply is minimally "no".

2. If you do not allow after-hours or weekend work in your office, and you believe this is not a one-time request or that it is good form to share the building policy then the reply is "no per the building hours policy".

3. If your building does not have a policy, but you have a cleaning crew coming in at 2:00 PM, make the reply "yes, between the hours of 9:00 AM and 1:30 PM".

4. If your building has a policy that you are bending or excluding, make the reply "yes, this is an exception due to the building policy of no after hours work". (Let's hope you own the building if you are making this exception!)

5. If you have no parameters on the request and use of the building for the planning meeting, simply state "yes", and let it be.

With all these examples, it is clear "maybe" or "I'll try" or "we'll see" are not needed. Just remember, saying yes when you mean no, or saying yes unconditionally when there is a condition or parameters, leads to frustration and miscommunication...mostly on your part.

Similarly, with so many people down on themselves and others, lead by example and resist using phrases like "I am not good at that", or "I cannot afford that", or "I would never be able to do that". Statements like this are full of negative self-talk and *what is not* rather than the can do...

Sure, not everything is a fit for one's strengths or one's budget, but that is no reason to shut down or shout out about it. Instead, when something is not your strength, consider stating it like "This is new to me and I am learning how to...", or "Because I have not been exposed to this before, XYZ is something of a good challenge for me". Additionally, when financial constraints are present, use "That is not a fit for my financial plans right now", or "Investing in that is not a match for my goals at this time".

Is it that they convey the same thing? Yes and no...you state something about you, yes; and no you don't depict yourself in a lack of interest or out of control position, you positively affirm the things you are doing.

It surely is interesting how acceptable someone saying "I'm trying to XYZ" is? What I mean is, we often nod and smile after hearing "I am trying to balance my work/life better", or "I am trying to be more patient", or even "I am trying to get better at names", when in fact, what we are really thinking (if we are engaged fully in that conversation) is that's lame..."you're trying"...I'll see how that works for you. Right? No? If not, then you are likely simply a "Try-er", too!

Try-ers are people who do not fully commit to things, engage totally or even make a true effort. Try-ers want an excuse for what might not go well.

Try-ers are fearful…of disappointing you, themselves, or someone else along the way.

Consider this, please: how many times does someone actually show up after he/she tells you he/she "might" or "will try" to join a function, group, or party? It is so infrequent; you will likely have few recollections of it occurring.

As a matter of fact, I prefer invitations/requests only offer a yes or no reply. Some of the wonderful and convenient online resources for invitations and announcements provide the cowardly "maybe", which is just a more direct form of "I'll try", or "I'm waiting to see if I get a better offer". I consider every maybe or "I'll try" to be a no, and write off that person as a committed or potentially committed attendee. If, in fact someone replies "maybe" or "I'll try" often enough, they are best served to be removed from my invitation list…and yours, too. By continuing to include them, you are forcing their weak position to another point of non-committal, non-truth where they are not strong enough to say "no, thank you", and rather give the lame, often insulting "I'll try" or "maybe".

If you are the "Try-er" in your group, you have created a false sense of honesty and openness with your friends/colleagues because your word is devalued. Each time you give a weak response or offer a weak statement voluntarily in conversation, you are feeding the other people's conscious or subconscious notions that you are, in fact, not in control of your decisions, focus, or time.

Wow! All that from a simple "I'll try"? Yes. Be
smart, straight-forward, and honest with people
when asked for a response or reply. I have heard
people rationalize "try-er" behavior as they do not
want to be rude, or they do not want to hurt other
people's feelings…really? How is it kind,
thoughtful, or real to suggest you will make an
effort, when in fact, you will not? Your character
and self-respect should be worth more to you. And,
if that is not the case, the people with whom you are
surrounding yourself may warrant a higher degree
of professional and personal thoughtfulness based
on their character.

So, what do you replace your wishy-washy verbiage
with when you are tempted to "try"? I say stop
trying, and start doing. A few scenarios are
outlined here:

When you would like to do something, yet do not
have all the details, say "I am saying no at this
point, as I am not in a position to say yes. As soon
as I have the details on XYZ (the babysitter, the
guests I have coming in, my work schedule, etc.), I
will get back to you. And, then, actually get back to
that person (minimally five days prior to the
event…see Chapter 41 for further details).

If though, you are just not interested, resist
providing excuses, and state "No, thank you.", or
"No, and thank you for asking.", and let it be. If the
person/people want to know the reason, they are
crossing the line. At that point, you owe them
nothing.

In the case where you are doing something new, such as learning a language, engaging in a new endeavor, etc., it is suggested that you convey that by saying "I am in the process of learning beginning Spanish", which is strong and clear, as opposed to verbalizing "I am trying to learn beginning Spanish", as that is nearly hopeless and less than positive. Another way to express something similar is by saying "I am taking classes in beginning Spanish on Mondays and Wednesdays." The ideal way to say it shows direction and offers solid information to those who are listening.

Imagine if you are trying to finish this book, think again, and be *in the process of* reading the entire book! With language and approaches in place, know that what you say will become what people expect. I often say you teach people the way to treat you, so please teach them with words of meaning and courtesy, so in turn, they'll know how to treat you similarly. Thank you!

LUNDBERGism

Be a bit courageous today...do or say something you would not normally say...or have the courage to not say or do something that may hurt another person. Courage is not all about bravery and heroics...it is about being willing to do something that is challenging or uncomfortable, and believing it was the correct thing to do for everyone involved.

Chapter 2
Why, Oh Why, Question Bug?

"The uncreative mind can spot wrong answers, but it takes a very creative mind to spot wrong questions." ~ Anthony Jay

WHY is it that we feel defensive when asked some questions? Believe it or not, the inquiry you just read as the chapter title may have already jump-started your defenses! How is that? It is because the tiny little word WHY has so many implications - and most of them are, unfortunately, negative.

Imagine we are at a local coffee shop and I ask you WHY did you get a tea instead of a latte? In asking that, my eyes will likely squint, one side of my lip will raise, my voice tone will intensify and the emphasis in the question will be on the WHY as well as LATTE - implying there is something wrong with the choice you made. While I may genuinely just be curious, the word WHY creates an environment of defense - even when we are just grabbing a coffee! Imagine what it does with family or in your professional exchanges, in meetings, or one-on-one!

So, what is the solution? Do nothing? Of course not - there is a simple and readily available option! Whenever you are thinking or asking WHY, substitute it for WHAT or HOW. In other words, that same question at the coffee shop becomes

HOW did you choose flavored tea?, or WHAT do you like about your tea?, which creates a conversation and a smooth exchange.

The appropriate use of why is in explaining, rather than questioning. Imagine rarely asking why and often offering why. That situation is demonstrated in "The reason I recommend (the why) a tea, is because it is low fat, refreshing and tasty – hot or cold." Not asking WHY is unexpected, kind, and allows you to learn of reasoning and perspective rather than raising people's defenses or simply receiving shrugs of "I dunno".

When someone (who has not read this tip) asks you WHY, just think to yourself WHAT lead me to this choice, or HOW did I arrive here before responding (not reacting). By doing this, you will temper your reply with calm and focus, getting the conversation directed in a positive and less-defensive fashion than the WHY, WHY, WHY back-and-forth. After the process of WHAT or HOW internally, keep it positive by sharing the sentiment verbally with WHAT and HOW…and then remember to ask the other person a follow-up question that encourages him or her to stay on the healthy and courteous path of conversation rather than interrogation!

Still, ask, ask, ask…in every situation! It is rare that someone regrets asking a question, yet often it is heard and thought that someone wishes he/she did ask something…even if it is/was just one more thing.

The old adage that there is no dumb question is true...with the exception that the truly dumb question is the one left unasked!

So, without apologies or hesitation, please proudly and firmly ask quick, direct, thoughtful questions. And then, enjoy and learn/grow from the answers!

Really, test it...look in the mirror and ask a "why" question, and watch your face distort and hear your voice accuse. After that, stay in the mirror and ask a "how" or "what" question, and see the softness and openness in your voice and face.

Keep your communication direct and without a wrongly-perceived attack by resisting "why" questions and replacing them with the "what" or "how" varieties.

LUNDBERGism

"Why?" questions evoke defense, while "What?" and "How" inquiries create conversations.

Chapter 3
20/20 x 2 Vision...From the Inside Out...

"The only thing worse than being
blind is having sight but no vision."
~ Helen Keller

How many times in a day or week do you see
people who look good, say something significant,
make an impact? OFTEN, right?

So, turn it around, how many times in a day or week
do you tell people who look good that you like how
he/she looks, tell people how insightful they were
after they said something significant, how their
impression was lasting after they made an impact?
NOT OFTEN, right?

What makes that gap?

Isn't it fair to say we have 20/20 vision from the
outside going in, but that we do not make the
time/effort to share 20/20 vision from the inside
out? If we did, that would be what I propose
here...20/20 x 2 Vision!

Implement this...within the first 20 seconds of
seeing someone or hearing someone, share one
thing, something with him/her that you like. That
something may be a firm handshake, spectacular
shoes, a beautiful tie, a warm smile...anything that
you genuinely like...and tell him/her about it.
Again, this is about the other person, and not you,
so do not go past the 20 second rule for sharing
either - it should not take you more than 20 seconds

to offer your glowing opinion. Next, each week, spend 20 minutes thinking about things you appreciate about others...something someone did or said and then, finally, spend a full 20 minutes writing people a handwritten note about their lasting impression as a result of what they did or said.

Expect nothing in return. If you get a thank you, that is wonderful. You did not share to get back, you shared because you sincerely thought or felt it, so there is no wrong answer from the person receiving your praise...know that. If though, a person disagrees, or says "this old thing" when you state your 20 seconds, just look him/her in the eye and repeat the compliment and move on. People who are not used to compliments and recognition may be uncomfortable. This is an opportunity to appreciate that in him/her and build his/her confidence subtly over time. At the same time, keep this in mind when you are receiving comments of recognition and refrain from negating the compliment by responding in kind or simply with a "thank you".

20/20 x 2 Vision is something that has nothing to do with sight, but so much to do with vision...try it...your view...and outlook, will clearly improve!

Chapter 4
Giving Thanks

"Appreciation is a wonderful thing. It makes what is excellent in others belong to us as well." ~ Voltaire

Thankfulness is something we tend to talk about and celebrate primarily in November in The United States of America. Still, thankfulness and appreciation for an act or abundance need not be reserved for days when turkey is traditionally served.

Regardless of your religion, position in life, or state of mind, often we are with others in groups around events and/or celebrations. When with others during special occasions, holidays, or every day, simply be thankful for them this way:

State his/her name (or nickname...it's okay with family/friends...avoid nicknames in business), You make me thankful for you because of your (attribute) and you inspire me to (their inspiration to you). Thank you.

Example I:
Danielle, you make me thankful for you because of your creative wit and you inspire me to be playful. Thank you.

Example II (with varied verbiage):
Steve, you make me thankful for your generosity and you make me want to be a giving person as well. Thank you.

Example III (letting someone know you acted as a result of them/their inspiration):
Carol, you make me thankful for you because you taught me to listen well and because of you, I became a Big Sister. Thank you.

Example IV (a strictly professional affiliation):
John, you make me thankful for your loyalty and because of your referrals, you have been a part of my business/sales growth. Thank you.

Note that the word "I" is not used as the first word (or really much at all). This is to ensure the other person knows it is about him or her and for him or her. Keep you thankful, and that other person in the forefront of the message and thankfulness.

Go ahead, use one or all of these with people for whom you are thankful...on a special day...or any day...and see how it makes a difference for you and the person with whom you shared!

LUNDBERGism

Find something, anything, to be happy about, grateful for, or even be in awe of today...and let that make your day early and often!

Chapter 5
Directing, Talking, or Communicating? The Choice is Yours!

"The art of communication is the language of leadership." ~ James Humes

Have you ever wondered what makes some people seem to "get you" while others do not? Many of us have experienced that latter sensation and usually chalk it up to the other person, right? Please consider that at times in our exchanges, we are directing, at other times we are talking, and better yet, there are times, hopefully often, when we are truly communicating. So, what is the difference?

When we are directing, we are giving a firm/set opinion, telling people what to do and/or ignoring things around us. In this case, some people will follow us, or rather, succumb to our influence or direction because he/she has no opinion, the other person does not engage in conflict, or, sadly, simply because that person is our child, or works for us!

If we move up the exchange ladder (and it is but a rung), we begin talking. This is less offensive than directing, yet we are still sharing opinions, telling our side and generally ignoring the other person/people's view. What makes it more tolerable is that we are not being bossy, rather just insensitive or insincere in an attempted or supposed conversation.

When we communicate, we are in a full, live exchange. We are offering ideas and are interested in others. We share an opinion and may not change it, and even though that is the case, we still listen and consider the other side of the argument or an opposing opinion. Communication involves a recognition and appreciation that people are different, and that fact alone, is okay. True communication even has the dynamic of sharing things in different ways with different people and personality types...in other words, the message and meaning is the same, the approach, tone and/or words are altered slightly for impact and results.

While you may be great at having an opinion and speaking aloud or in front of people, next time you have the opportunity, which will be often since the majority of life is impromptu, challenge yourself to not direct, not even just talk, but rather to communicate! The way to ensure communication is to ask questions and then engage in listening. Offer opinion(s) with thought and awareness of others and commit to respond and not just react (as mentioned previously in my writings). This empowers you to be in a position to learn and share as well as become an effective communicator. The best communicators do not share things in the way that suits or hits them, rather in a way that is best received by the person or people with whom they are communicating.

Remember, it is your choice, make the right one for you and your audience of one or many, as communication is communication is communication, regardless of topic or audience size!

Chapter 6
Seven Steps to Email Wow!

"It has become appallingly obvious
that our technology has exceeded
our humanity." ~ Albert Einstein

Please embrace the idea that anything written in an email can, and likely will, be forwarded, printed, or minimally saved...indefinitely!

With people getting multiple emails each day, how does your email get read?

Remember that people have choices for what to do with their time, and reading emails fully becomes "optional" to a lot of individuals, and even within some company/corporate cultures. So, to set yourself apart and increase your "readability" factor with outgoing emails, keep in mind that most everyone's favorite topic is himself or herself, and not you...meaning appeal to them rather than just what you want to "say" in the message.

Here are seven simple tips to effective emailing:

1. Have a subject line that is capitalized, and reads like a book title. Do you inform and intrigue people with your six words-or-less subject line? Your subject is not the start of the email message, rather it is a way to let the reader know what he/she is opening. Think of it as an opportunity for someone to choose to open or

delete your message. Keep in mind that often others can/will see someone's emails, so while subject lines should be informative, they need not be blatant. If say, someone owes you $50, an appropriate subject line is Repayment Requested This Week versus That $50 You Owe Me's Due. Thoughtfulness and consideration go a long way in life, and email subject lines are not different. Many people read emails on the go and/or on hand-held devices, so the subject line is like a movie trailer…it assists in determining its worth and the interest to the potential viewer. Subject lines are not, however, intended to be the start of an email. Subject lines like "Today" are weak, as that could mean many things…clearly not about tomorrow, but other than that, it is vague. At the same time "In reference to your talking with me today, we have to reschedule" is too long and part of the body of an email. A sound solution would be "Rescheduling 3:00 PM Meeting to 4:00 PM". Also, when a topic changes in an email exchange, make the subject line fit the information in the message instead of just bouncing back and forth on an old subject line. Consider not opening messages without subject lines for 24 hours...and communicate that...I do! If someone cares enough about the message in the email, he/she will take time to address the "book cover" first!

2. Have a greeting that is simple, and includes minimally the recipient's name. Something like "Hi Tina.", or "Hello Tom!" both work. If you do not want to be as lengthy, start with "Tina:", or "Tom:". Not using someone's name is one way to prove your message is about you, and

not the reader (if he/she even reads your messages!)!

3. Briefly lead-in or bridge, which gets you connected to the reader (such as "Thank you for your prompt response", or "What a great idea you shared in the meeting"). Refrain from beginning your communication with "I" and be mindful of the number of "I"s as well. Starting a paragraph with "I want to talk with you about the Murphy account" works, and "Because the Murphy account is important to both of our success, let's please schedule a meeting to discuss it", is even better. It is preferred for being a) inclusive; b) to the point, and c) informative.

4. Get to the point of the message or request. Be mindful not to fall into the mindset of Ashleigh Brillian when it was said, "Inform all the troops that communications have completely broken down." If you have information to share, consider bullets or numbers. This is visually pleasing, and bullets indicate all items are of equal importance, where numbering things indicates a flow/process or priority. Choose your differentiators with intention. This is not a quick communication where all manners are neglected. With any communication, strive to be concise, provide answers to questions asked and pre-empt further questions. Aside from a greeting and closing line/paragraph, email communication is designed to provide information in three paragraphs or less (and that does not mean just roll on and on in one to keep to a three paragraph "rule"!). If information takes more than the three key parts of the

communication, perhaps it should be an attachment or a presentation.

5. Offer to own the follow-up (something like "should I not hear from you by Tuesday, I will go ahead and book the meeting for 4:00 PM at your office, and send you a confirmation").

6. Go for the quick close ("Warm Regards", "Kindly").

7. Include your full signature with your contact information.

Should an email string go back and forth more than twice, it is time for either a phone call or meeting. Email is not designed to replace actual interaction or face-to-face communication; rather, it is to expedite the process and aid in improved communication. In this vein, avoid "reply all" unless it is requested. People's lives are full and simply deleting your "bulk" message requires time and energy.

It follows that you want to keep your emails fact-based. As mentioned earlier, these electronic communications will be kept or forwarded, so the emotional part of opinion is best avoided. Choose your words by giving consideration to the fact that the recipient cannot know your "mood" when you crafted your message. Tone is something that is misinterpreted in emails on a daily, if not moment-to-moment, basis. The reader's perspective, what the reader will think, is also not something you can predict, so provide information in bulleted form where appropriate, and offer a timetable so that expectations are not over-looked. This means allow time for reading and response. Sending a 5:55 PM Friday meeting request email for an 8:00 AM Monday meeting is not realistic and not considerate (use the phone...or, better yet, just plan ahead!).

Keep copies of what you send in your sent file for future reference and know that when you send an email, it is professional, friendly, to the point, appropriate, and useful for both the recipient and you.

Something controversial and often challenging to do, is to resist the oh-so-common bounce-back "thank you" email. When someone has sent you something, let them know you appreciate it when you see them. If it is part of the course of business, technology is such that server crashes and lost emails are rare.

While I am a huge proponent of appreciation, a "thank you in advance" in your closing paragraph covers that and speaking face-to-face after the fact keeps email communication from overshadowing courtesy and speaking to one another. For example, to bring together the mentioned changes for emailing, on the next page is a full message:

Subject: Rescheduling 3 PM Meeting to 4 PM

Hi Stewart!

Here's hoping all is well with you! Because the Murphy account is important to both of our success, let's please continue to work on our parts and meet to discuss it.

An event has me out of the office Tuesday until mid-day, making 4:00 PM best for an hour discussion on:

- Approach
- Division of Labor
- Results
- Next Steps

Thank you in advance for your flexibility. Out of respect for your full calendar, if I do not hear back from you by tomorrow at 6:00 PM, I'll book a conference room under the guise that Tuesday at 4:00 PM works for you.

Regards,

Debbie Lundberg, MBA, Certified Life Coach
"Committed to applied knowledge, growth, fun & ROI."
Debbie@DebbieLundberg.com

813.494.4438

Debbie Lundberg Life & Business Coaching
"Partnering to Develop, Inspire, Train & Coach"
www.DebbieLundberg.com

813.835.0196

Be brief, be direct, and be gone so that your reader's time is respected, and you make a compelling reason for the reader to respond…and read your future communication!

Chapter 7
What We Are NOT Saying...

"Deafness has left me acutely aware
of both the duplicity that language is
capable of and the many
expressions the body cannot hide."
~ Terry Galloway

Whether intentional or not, each of us "says" things
without words each and every day. Looking at
someone means something completely different
than not looking at someone...and to top it all off,
how we look at them has a great impact as well!

Even our very presence conveys a message...in our
contact with other people, it is impossible not to
communicate. Various and frequent research
indicates an estimated 70 - 93% of the
communication between people takes place through
non-verbal or misinterpreted experiences.

If this is the case, we express most of our feelings in
a non-verbal way...so what is all the *noise*
about????

Well, while we do not talk non-stop, we do give out
signals continuously when we are in someone else's
company, and, it is useful to look at the different
levels on which we communicate. In general, each
of us, and all of us, communicate on two levels,

minimally, at the same time. These two levels are informational and rapport building. Our verbiage and word choice provide information, and our conveyance of tone and/or interest drive or repel rapport.

While talking about something when we speak with other people, it is necessary to be clear about a particular topic or subject. This is the information in/of the conversation. In the informational exchange, we speak, or convey, the message. It is usually easiest to convey the content of a message through spoken language. Due to the fact that the meaning of words, figures or data that we use have been agreed upon within the context of work or the situation, the informational state is one for inquiry, questions, and clarity. To understand the other person you want to speak his language and seemingly the message will be communicated clearly, but it is not that simple, is it?

Information and data are not the only things that we convey through communication. Through our words we give signals that indicate how we view the other person as well as how he should interpret our message. At the rapport building level, we express how we relate, and what the message means. It is challenging for us to express only in words exactly what we mean. How we feel about the other person is even more difficult to make clear. Words may come across harsher than they are meant to be interpreted. To make our feelings and intentions clear, we therefore, prefer an expressive process/approach. As a result, what is being expressed can be recognized in the gesture or signal solely. For example, winking has something to do with humor or playfulness, so even though the wink is not about the eye, and nothing is typically "said" with the wink, the two involved now "speak the same language".

So, please keep in mind that intent is not always conveyed. Your non-verbal has a vernacular all of its own...and, knowing this allows us to make good, intentional choices regarding what we communicate...through our words and our actions.

With that, you are encouraged to use this information and perspective to in fact, walk the talk.

LUNDBERGism

It is often your demeanor and delivery, your look and the feel of an experience that will be remembered...even if the words somehow get "forgotten".

Chapter 8
No Apologies for these Four, Please...

"The best day of your life is the one on which you decide your life is your own. No apologies or excuses. No one to lean on, rely on, or blame. The gift is yours - it is an amazing journey - and you alone are responsible for the quality of it. This is the day your life really begins."
~ Bob Moawad

While I am a huge proponent of excusing oneself and asking forgiveness when appropriate, there are four things which I believe there need not be apologies. These are:

1. For being intelligent/informed
2. For asking a question for clarification
3. For being right
4. For sharing emotion when it comes from the heart

When someone is smart/intelligent (not just "being smart"), there is an appropriateness in having a delicate combination of humility and pride. I hear people saying they are sorry for knowing something. There is no excuse for flaunting things. The truly intelligent person shares things for growth of self and others at nobody's expense, and therefore, no need for apology.

Similarly, not knowing something is not something for which an apology is warranted. When asking for clarification for learning and/or avoiding mistakes or oversights, the questions come solely from a place of desire to learn, and therefore, not from a place of needing any type of forgiveness.

If there is a situation where one has been challenged, and he/she is correct, there is also no need to apologize. Being right is not about someone else being wrong, so done with kindness and firmness is not only the best thing to do, it should be the only thing to do.

When one's voice quivers, shakiness in hands or body is apparent or even tears come, there is not a need to apologize if those emotions are from the heart. Sure, if someone uses emotions to manipulate people or get something undeserved, that is not alright, rather emotions that are real and heartfelt make someone both believable and vulnerable...and real.

If you are tempted to apologize for being intelligent, asking a question, being right, or sharing emotion when it comes from the heart, just take a breath, smile inside and know that you not only do not want to apologize, but that you should be proud of yourself for being you!

LUNDBERGism

While the difference in 2 and 4 may be 2, the difference in "to" and "for" is your perspective...are you letting things happen "to" you, or "for" you?

Chapter 9
Communication/Correspondence…
What to Use Where and When

"Good leaders must first become good servants." ~ Robert Greenleaf

Communication, or a version or ghost of it, happens on a regular basis, right? Not so fast! Data exchange or information dumping is provided frequently, but *effective* communication…carefully thought out sharing, is somewhat of a rarity.

The reasons we don't communicate as effectively as we can are many, and this tip is about the right formats for communicating.

Face-to-face is preferred. Preferred by whom, you might be thinking…preferred for the least amount of miscues, distractions, and oversights…preferred for results. Yes, it is the most time consuming, takes coordination and space, but it is the best because body language is the majority of communication, distractions are minimized when looking in one's eyes, and the recording and recapping of the commitments is immediate. If something is quick, it can be discussed in passing, but if more than two minutes is needed, schedule with someone with a time request. A time request is the amount of time needed…15 minutes, 30 minutes, 45 minutes, etc.

Voicemail is convenient, even tempting to use in place of the in-person conversation. This is not a solution in place of face-to-face. Voicemail is appropriate when someone is not available in person, or to quickly convey something of timeliness that is brief. Voicemails should be no longer than one minute, only when one or more of the parties is not on-site, and not done after hours only to avoid direct communication or to dump things on another person. When leaving a voicemail, provide slowly and clearly (as though someone has not heard it before) your name first, your phone number second, the brief message of only one topic per message third, your name again, and your number again. This allows for commuters to be able to retrieve your name and number quickly if they are saving the message. How nice is that? Imagine if you did not have to listen to an entire message just to get a number!

Email is definitely not the shield, so to speak, that it has become for people to resist face-to-face interactions. Emails should be no more than four paragraphs in length, are to address one topic each with a subject line that discloses the topic clearly, and changed in replies if the content of the email is different from the original subject line. Remember, emails can be forwarded and/or kept – figure they will, and be wise in your tone, word selection, and message.

Texting is the most recent form of "communication", and it has a short-hand language that is unique to texters. Sure, texting is quick (so long as you have figured out your thumb coordination if you have an older phone), but it is used primarily socially. If this is used professionally, it is the least recommended form of exchange…reserved for mostly one-way communication like to state where you are, the meeting is still on, the meeting is not on, etc. The reason texting is appropriate is only to get a message sent when the person is not available to answer a phone. Since many people are driving when receiving updates, that is reason alone not to request replies on texts.

For all forms of primary communication (everything prior to texting), have an agenda, share that agenda, stay focused on the topic, resist multi-tasking during the interaction, provide a time guideline and respect that time commitment, and provide a recap of ownership of items following the interaction if there are assignments. By following these communication guidelines, you can/will avoid misinterpretation and a perceived lack of communication or overload of information by knowing what to use when and where.

Chapter 10
Offer Choices, Get Prepared

"We can try to avoid making choices by doing nothing, but even that is a decision." ~ Gary Collins

Have you ever found you ask someone what she or he wants to do only to hear something completely different from what you want to do...or worse yet..."I dunno"?

If so, that is not the fault (not that we are assessing blame here!) of the person with whom you are interacting, rather it is an opportunity for you to change your approach. Incorporate the process of offering choices to the other person in order to be prepared for expectations and experiences.

For example, if you have parts of a paper or report due, ask someone something like "Do you prefer to handle the report or the graphs?", or "Would you like to take the lead, or have me spearhead this?". Similarly, if you are looking to lock down a time/date/location for a meeting or event, please consider asking "Do you want to schedule the meeting at 2 o'clock today or 3 o'clock tomorrow?", or "Is Thursday or Friday better for you?", "Would you like to meet in person or via conference video?" For each reply, note it, and elaborate (not to get irritating or irritated, for that matter, instead, it is for clear options.)

On a personal note, this happens with making plans for the night or where to go for a meal. Here are some phrasing examples that may assist: "Do you want to go out for dinner or stay in?" Imagine the person opts to go out, then ask "Do you want Thai or French food?" Whichever is selected, you can follow up with "Would you rather go to dinner at 6:30 PM or 7:00 PM?" The final note is something like "Okay, so I'll make reservations for 7:00 PM for the French restaurant downtown!" Now, *that* is being prepared to know what is anticipated for the evening!

<Slobification Snippet>
You surely do not want to retort with "Oh, I really wanted to eat earlier, and Thai food sounds so much lighter to me." That would not only be unfair, it would create a 'can't-win-for-losing' scenario for your potential dinner companion!

Make the options things that are fine with you regardless of the selection made. This ensures you will not be shocked by the reply, and you will be including others in the final decision. Sure, someone can say neither, but watch, it happens rarely, as the choices are presented calmly, pleasantly, and in a sincere offer of going along with whichever is selected. So instead of asking what, include a choice, and watch the decisions get made swiftly and enjoyably in most cases!

LUNDBERGism

Having a plan is good...being prepared is even better! Something can go wrong or change in a plan (even the most thorough plan), and if you are prepared, that means you can adjust, change, and even improve things based on your preparation and the situation!

Chapter 11
Help! The Best Way to Request Assistance

"Act as if what you do makes a difference. It does." ~ William James

From a formal perspective, in Webster's II New Revised Dictionary, help is defined as "To give relief to", where assist is defined as "To aid, to enable another/teammate". Shifting to the informal or gut level response to the words, help suggests someone cannot complete something without your intervening, to many people, and assist means collaborate or serve.

If you have been to one of my seminars or been a coaching/training client individually or through your company, you have no doubt heard me suggest you consider resisting the phrase "How may I help you?" This is because most people do not feel or think they need "help". So, when you ask "How may I help you?" you are sending their minds and senses to a place where they do not believe they would like to go.

It is okay, and even suggested, though, that you do request assistance or help. Yes, as I have previously written, your asking for help is entirely different than offering help. How so? Well, asking for assistance and/or help is stating you are aware you are not completing something or able to accomplish something on your own or in the time frame you prefer. When you ask someone for help, you are not putting them in a position where they are assessing your need...you have stated it.

There are many different approaches to requesting help. Most of us have experienced the "I need you to XYZ" approach, which is really not a request, rather a demand, and that is not recommended. Additionally, we have likely all experienced someone struggling and not asking for help, per se, rather moaning and groaning and then letting us know they can "lend a hand". This, too, is not recommended, for it is not direct, and puts the onus on the other person.

The recommended way to ask for assistance is to give the reasoning first and make a clear, direct request that has limits and is specific.

For example, let's say you want to have someone help you move a desk that is big and heavy. An option for asking for help is to inquire "Since this desk is big and I want to move it across the hall, are you willing to help me for 15 minutes to do that this afternoon?"

Another approach is to get help with something that is unfamiliar. Imagine there is a large room where party decorating is needed, you may want to approach people who are experienced in decorating with "because you are good at decorating, will you please help me get the room looking like a fun and festive party later today? I anticipate it taking an hour of our time."

At work, you may have read or heard me say there are no favors, so rather than asking for help with "Do me a favor..." just allow for the information to flow with a time element and enough necessary detail. If you want a report for the past three months of sales from a sales team member consider "since you have access to the sales figure, will you please help me by pulling the last three months of data and arrange it by XYZ criteria before Friday's 2:00 PM meeting and send it to me in soft copy?"

If you are thinking "I am not bothered by or offended by someone asking me if I need help", you are not alone...you are just among the fewest personality types of people. It is fine to ask for help, I simply encourage you not to offer to help. If there is a greater portion of people who either consciously or subconsciously find help something that is not appealing, there is reason enough to alter your language to assist (or serve), as that verbiage will not resonate with varied personalities as demeaning or suggestive of error/fault.

So, the next time you want to enthusiastically offer "help", simply replace that with "assist", and be mindful of the response. Over time, you will find more and more people taking you up on your aid and enabling...and that is a win for teaming, communication and productivity no matter how you phrase it. By your kind tone and your recognition of the other person's position and time, help will be on the way!

Chapter 12
If You Have Nothing Nice to Say…

"A little Consideration, a little Thought for Others, makes all the difference." ~ Winnie the Pooh

Has it ever happened that someone has been speaking in short-hand, jargon or even a foreign language around you? If you are at all interested in communicating with the other people, how did you feel…what did you think?

With some close friends or colleagues, we often develop our own code or language, so to speak. While that may seem convenient and convey closeness or the sharing of the same page on topics/issues, it is not appropriate to use it around new friends, team members, clients or vendors, in that the language will only alienate the others and isolate you. What may appear to insulate you from someone "cracking your code" is just a disregard for communication and inclusion.

Similarly, in particular in work environments or clubs, a jargon of acronyms or abbreviations develops. When others are around, they too are subject to a sense of not belonging or secrecy.

The ultimate is when languages other than the most common in the environment are being used. This is disconcerting because there is a sense of being mocked or wrongly interpreted in those cases. While it could be easier to speak with someone in a particular language, if that is not a known language of a third party or the intended language of the conversation, presentation, call or situation, do not veer from the original language. From nail salons to major corporations, there are blog and complaint sites stating people will not continue to do business where, whether it was true or not, people were rudely ignored or disrespected with a language that was unfamiliar to the situation.

While you may be comfortable talking in quips, jargon or other languages, stick with a full command of one language and allow the others in the conversation to communicate rather than feel a sense that you are there to alienate or intimidate.

LUNDBERGism

Take nothing for granted...someone or something that was here yesterday may not be here today...be expressive, show/share your feelings, and make the most of all you have!

Chapter 13
Lose "Honestly" and "Truthfully" to Gain Respect

"Men are respectable only as they respect." ~ Ralph Waldo Emerson

What? Can that chapter title, "Lose 'Honestly' and 'Truthfully' to Gain Trust" be right? No way...

Yes, way...

When people preface statements or opinions with "To be honest with you", "Truthfully", "To tell you the truth", or even "Honestly", it implies other statements and/or opinions may not be the truth or from an honest perspective. Mentally people consider the notion of 'what, you haven't been in the past?'...hmmmmmm...and then, imagine statements following ones with "To be honest with you", "Truthfully", "To tell you the truth", or "Honestly" that now don't have one of those as a lead in, does that mean you now are not being honest or truthful?

Sure, these verbal crutches, as I call them, are intended for emphasis and impact, but they do not enhance or gain trust, rather they subtly imply you may not have been as forthright in the past, but, wow, now you are, so the receiver should 'listen carefully'.

Instead of "To be honest with you", "Truthfully", "To tell you the truth", or "Honestly", consider no words (a pause) or "I find", "Based on what I know, it appears", "With these circumstances, my position is". There are other options as well that may work to gain trust, too...it's just a funny thing that when we purport "honesty" and "truth", that is usually when people tend to question it!

For your best impression, keep those expressions like "To be honest with you", "Truthfully", "To tell you the truth", or even "Honestly" on the shelf and simply communicate without a preface to a statement or with something that doesn't work against you, and watch your trust with the person receiving the message grow...

Chapter 14
Say What You Mean & Mean What You Say!

"First learn the meaning of what you say, and then speak." ~ *Epictetus*

Have you ever been on a plane or with a tour group in a new area and the leader/representative says "I'd like to welcome you to XYZ!"? Surely that sounds familiar…it is similar to when someone inquires "May I ask you a question?" Verbiage such as this does not assert anyone as saying what is meant and meaning what is said, instead, it just adds time, words, and no additional value to the communication. Often these are odd habits, and other times they are simply "verbal crutches".

How so? What…you would like to, but you cannot, or you will not? And, how many times has anyone refused someone a question? If they are going to deny responding, asking permission is not likely going to alter the disposition of the speaker. To best demonstrate, here are the suggested changes to what is mentioned above:

"I'd like to welcome you to XYZ!" becomes simply "Welcome to XYZ!" The "I'd like to" part of it, is just the speaker speaking…and saying nothing. This type of statement is prevalent in, ironically, thank you notes/correspondence in the form of "I'd like to thank you for XYZ", so, go ahead and thank the person! The "I'd like to" makes the statement about you…and not the other person for whom you are (supposedly) showing gratitude. Resist starting any communication with "I", completely lose the "I'd like to", and state clearly what is happening or that which is appreciated. Your goal is to demonstrate that you are less self-focused and most sincere.

"May I ask you a question?" is easily converted to "What is XYZ?", or "How did you arrive at XYZ?". Asking permission to ask a question is redundant in the fact that the positioning of the statement is what you just did…you asked a question (and please remember speakers are often thinking 'you just did' in response to the hollow inquiry)! While it may seem polite and courteous, it is just a filler…adding zero value, so be kind, refrain from asking questions in a why format (by using a what or a how to position the question) and go ahead…ask…and see/hear the useful and direct replies you receive!

With a bit of a different tone, what is with the "No, I agree." statement? What? You are stopping me, or you are halting the conversation to state you agree? "No, I know" is another one. These are similar to people saying "um" or "like" a lot. They add no value, and are not only distracting, they border on insulting when repeated at such an insistent rate or tone (as though they have value or some sort of approval in them). It has been said that silence is golden, and I dare say silence is appropriate…especially when the words you are choosing consciously or not, are limiting, if not irritating, and/or ultimately alienating you audience.

The last set of verbal inconsistencies are "always" and "never". Interesting enough, most of the time when people use the words "always" or "never", they are highlighting something in conflict with the statement. An example is when somebody states something like "I was eating a hamburger yesterday, and I *never* eat red meat". Another example is "I neglected to lock the gate and the dog got out, and I *always* lock the gate before I leave the yard". The substitution of "consistently", "usually", "often", and/or "regularly" for "always" and the change from "never" to "rarely" or "seldom" will allow for the realities of life that keep us from doing things exactly the same way each time we take action. The examples given would then read "I was eating a hamburger yesterday, and I *rarely* eat red meat", and "I neglected to lock the gate and the dog got out, and I *usually* lock the gate before I leave the yard". While the statements may seem like they are the same, in fact they are just similar enough to demonstrate the differences.

Some, such as I, say the aforementioned pre-fillers encourage people not to listen to us, since word choices that are like those in the first paragraph, become expected, anticipated, and even ignored. It is fair to say each of us has felt as though people were not listening or we were not being heard, so to create the best environment for listening and being heard, say what you mean and mean what you say.

LUNDBERGism

Be true to yourself, and ensure your voice is being heard…nobody will speak it for you, or quite the way you do.

Chapter 15
Please Wait for the Beep, and Leave a Message…

"My life is my message."
~ Mahatma Gandhi

So often a phone call results in an outgoing message followed by a beep, that most of us leave at least one message each day…if not up to 100! Leaving a message is both an art and a skill. Wanting to leave a good, communicative, brief message is something I would guess few think about…therefore, few accomplish…

Prior to phoning someone, whether you get them live on the phone or not, have an agenda…yes, that is right, an agenda! The reason for the agenda is to give you direction. This need not be written, just keep in mind that if there are more than two topics, it is highly recommended that you do at least jot down the main topics.

Upon that familiar fourth ring that typically precedes a voicemail request, stop and listen. Someone may have clear directions/suggestions for having issues addressed, so be present and accountable by taking in the person's message prior to leaving your own.

When you do hear the beep, take a breath and recall that the other person, who will later hear your message (likely while doing something else as well), has no idea what your intent or even your message is. Knowing that, similar to the email communication tip, offer a greeting with the person's name followed by your name and your full 10-digit phone number. Say your phone number as though you are relaying it for the first time…in case the person is hearing it for the first time. Follow that with a brief description of what your call is related to (see agenda). Ask for a type of reply…written or verbal, and thank the person in advance for getting back to you on or before a date or time. Even though you have already stated your name and your number, wrap up the message with appreciation and (again) your name and number.

An example of all of this together is:

"Hi Marty, this is Debbie Lundberg…calling from 813.494.4438. Thank you for the message. Your follow through is appreciated and I will be able to attend a meeting on the 7th or the 10th. To discuss the details, please contact me via phone or email any afternoon this week. Again, Marty, this is Debbie Lundberg at 813.494.4438. Should your schedule not permit a response, I will follow up by the 4th. Thank you and make it a wonderful evening! Bye."

Leaving a message like this allows for the greatest possibility of a prompt reply based on your being thoughtful and thorough while maintaining a respectful brevity and directness. If someone is listening on the run, so to speak, he or she will only have to replay the first part of the message to get your number later since you have been so kind as to slowly and clearly state your name and number at the beginning. Imagine how much easier it would be if each of the messages you received each day were left on your voicemail this way!

Chapter 16
Positive Brevity

"The obstacles you face are... mental barriers which can be broken by adopting a more positive approach." ~ Clarence Blasier

How often do you ask someone "how are you?" in passing...only to have them actually tell you how they are...meaning they stopped and proceeded to share with you the ins and outs of their recent health and wellness concerns, or details about their family vacation, etc.? Of course it is not that you wouldn't sometime want to hear all of that, and really, it is not that person's misstep for sharing, for after all, you asked!

This is not a suggestion you erase the question "how are you?" from your life forever, rather, if you like to ask someone "how are you?", please only inquire in that way when you have at least 10 minutes to invest in that conversation. This question is a legitimate introduction to a conversation, and when used with that intention, will provide opportunities for relationship building and care instead of a rhetorical, thoughtless statement or brief exchange.

So, what to do? If you are in a hurry, simply say "hello" or "good morning" or "good afternoon" to someone you encounter. Additionally, you may offer "what a beautiful day!" if it is, in fact, a beautiful day. The point of this is to offer only an observation, and I recommend only positive ones, to someone else.

If you do want to take a moment or two, keep it positive by asking "what is going well for you?" or "what is going well today" or "what are you enjoying right now?". Eight or nine out of ten people will reply with an answer to your direct question. The other one or two will either not have been listening and think you asked the traditional "how are you?", or might say "nothing", and if that is the case, just move forward with your day. If you are compelled to respond, make it a "surely you will turn it around" or something similar.

Remember to be sincere in each greeting, comment and question when interacting with someone. Say what you mean and watch the responses come in kind...direct, informative, and respectful...all because you were intentional in asking the right one-on-one opening question.

LUNDBERGism

If you remember to put your best foot forward consistently, each step, each day, can be part of a worthwhile and enjoyable "walk" of life!

Chapter 17
Get Specific

"No problem can be solved until it is reduced to some simple form. The changing of a vague difficulty into a specific, concrete form is a very essential element in thinking." ~ John Pierpont Morgan

Commitment is important in big and small things alike, as when there is a commitment, we rely on *action* following.

When someone makes a commitment to do something for you, your business or for him/herself, to be encouraging, ask him/her the following specific three things:

1. What makes this a priority for you?
2. What is your first step (or next step if it is in process)?
3. When are you taking that step?

These inquiries allow for:

1. Shared involvement/awareness.
2. Accountability for that person.
3. Your ability to follow through on the replies, and learn about/from the person.

This makes for a lively and informative conversation. There is no need for these questions to be like a battery or inquisition when they are legitimate, practical and relevant.

Either share your position along with the replies of the person questioned or afterward, offer your perspective and interpersonal sharing with respect.

By getting specific, you will also avoid miscommunication and/or missed deadlines...and know where you (both) stand.

LUNDBERGism

The opposite of being bold is not being drab, it is being indifferent. Be bold, be different, and take a stand for what you believe!

Chapter 18
Ask and You Shall Receive

"I like to listen. I have learned a great deal from listening carefully. Most people never listen." ~ Ernest Hemingway

If you are already a manager, become a leader, or enhance your leadership by asking each team member (note, I am not using "people" or "employee" rather "team member", for is inclusive) the following...regardless of how long he/she has been on your team:

1. What do you miss about your past employers? Listen for indications of guidelines, freedoms, etc.

2. What don't you miss about your past employers? Stay neutral...this is not where you are defending, rather gathering insight and information.

3. How do you like to be recognized?

4. When do you like to be recognized?

5. Is cash, a gift, or time off more important to you if there is budget allocated for recognition?

6. What keeps you happy here?

7. What is the best way for you to receive constructive criticism? Surely if the other questions had not been asked, this one would not have been either! Most people will respond with either a quick joke or laugh, as it is

surprising and awkward, or they'll tend to be thoughtful in their reply. The first response is due to discomfort. The second is because they either had not ever thought about it, or truly do not know. None of us love to be taught, but most everyone enjoys learning, so the concept of pre-planning the format/timing for learning is quite respectful, and in some ways daunting to people.

8. From what type of interaction do you learn best...written or verbal, informal or formal? (The natural follow up question is to ask how he/she learned that, if you like). While some things must be formally documented, if someone likes immediacy, respecting his/her way of processing will often be the most effective way to lead, assist in growth, and retain that person if that is your goal.

9. What either bothers you or makes you question your continuing to work here?

10. What is one thing I can do to become an improved leader for, and with you?

If you are not the team's formal, titled leader, still consider asking 1-4, 6, 8 and 9, as you will learn much and grow in your listening, learning, and leadership as a result.

Using these 10 things, or the seven suggested above, will show interest, humility and forward focus.

These can be asked in a review, casually over lunch, or in the form of a survey. Just remember, if you survey a group, provide feedback within the month to show you paid attention and value the input.

LUNDBERGism

If you want to get to know the team, get to know the individuals, and if you want to get to know the team, spend time with the individuals...

Chapter 19
How to Disagree Professionally and LAST

"I must respect the opinions of others even if I disagree with them." ~ Herbert Henry Lehman

A well-written opinion message allows for clarity and understanding (not to be confused with agreement). As long as you have an intent that is focused and clear while anticipating your audience, you will likely have success. Still, in order to be as well-prepared as possible, the following steps to effectively disagreeing agreeably will assist you in achieving just that!

1. Decide what you want to inspire: thoughts, exchange, debate…

2. Imagine various perspectives…regardless of your position.

3. Assess whether you have exposure, experience or expertise in the subject area and know that your audience will know that as well.

4. Use the LAST approach, including:
   Listen and have respect for the other person's opinion;
   Acknowledge: (what you have heard/read) for connection, and to show respect;
   Share one or two stories with facts and evidence that are compelling/interesting;
   Tell your opinion.

5. Create an outline and draft including an introduction L(Listen), A(Acknowledge), S(Share), and T(Tell).

6. Use proper vocabulary, punctuation, spelling, and tense without acronyms (unless used only after the full description), slang or colloquial references.

7. Be passionate about the topic without being emotional about potential conflicts.

8. Look forward to the replies/ideas that you may or may not have considered.

9. Know you may not change the person's mind, and that you still both have your opinion without there being a fight.

The steps above allow for a logical, calm, professional approach to sharing your opinion…whether others agree or not…and leaving room for making the relationship LAST.

LUNDBERGism

In life and in business, it is a performance test, and not just an endurance test!

Chapter 20
Steps 1 – 8 to Small Talk Success

"I know that you believe you
understand what you think I said, but
I'm not sure you realize that what you
heard is not what I meant."
~ Robert McCloskey

Small talk is part of life. It need not have a little
interest or enthusiasm. To enjoy small talk and be
effective, consider the following for
implementation:

1. Be likeable – not to be confused with being
   "like a bull". Go ahead, be the first to (delete
   say) greet other guests with a smile as you say
   "hello"!

2. Shake hands when you meet someone…even if
   you've met before or there are a lot of people
   around. Shaking hands stems from a ritual of
   trusting the other person had nothing hidden up
   his sleeve, like poison, in the "olden days", and
   as odd and germy as it may seem to do it today,
   it is still a professional courtesy (and even
   expectation) if you want to be taken seriously.
   Say your first and last name slowly to the
   person (even if you have met him or her before)
   so that you can save those "I'm bad with names,
   but good with faces" people.

3. Be mindful during introductions. Make the
   effort to remember names of those you meet,
   and use them readily. Be the person who

introduces new acquaintances to others so that you are seen as the connector.

4. Ask a direct, non-intimidating question like "how do you know the host?" if at a house party, or "what attracted you to this event?" if at a conference, so that the conversation begins on a positive reference point/perspective. Also, know what current events, movies, and books are being talked about. Have an opinion on them, but ask others their opinions first so as to not get confrontational right away.

5. Stay engaged verbally and with eye contact. Resist glancing around the room while others are talking to you, as it appears you are flighty and/or looking for a better opportunity elsewhere. Listen more than you talk if you are not there to be the entertainer/speaker.

6. If/when appropriate, present two business cards to the other person with the cards framed with your index finger and thumb...facing the full card to the recipient. If the other person reciprocates, look at the card and comment on something positive/interesting about the card. Put other cards in the same place you keep yours to show those received have the same value.

7. Watch monopolizing others. Be friendly, be memorable, and be moving on. Know when and how to exit a conversation by stating things like "it'll be great to speak more about this at another time, I'll follow up with you later this week via email" (if you will), or "surely there are a lot of people who want to meet you, so I will respect that and not monopolize your time.

It was a pleasure". Close with shaking the person's hand and using his/her name again.

8. Think like versus think. Often it is wonderful to seek another's outlook or opinion on an idea or project. Before asking a friend, colleague, team member, or superior about an idea or proposal, consider changing "what do you think about this?" to "what do you like about this?" Asking what one likes starts things off on a positive note, and will likely keep things moving in that direction. Following a lively discussion about what is right, per se, you can move on to "what you see as areas for change/improvement?" That question will show your interest, respect, and appreciation for input. Simply asking "what do you think" will get you all sorts of things that may be positive, may be negative, could border on self-serving or prove completely off-track, but begin with "what do you like", and watch/feel/hear the conversation stay on track!

Remember this tip with individuals and groups when you want to make it a likeable experience (which, of course not to be confused with someone or something being "Like-a-bull" with pushiness or stubbornness!).

LUNDBERGism

Do the things you do for others extraordinarily well instead of attempting to be an extraordinary person!

Chapter 21
Thinking Before Speaking?

"Love and doubt have never been on speaking terms." ~ Kahlil Gibran

Many people say "think before you speak", but what is it that we should be thinking? Perhaps you'll think about the following five concepts:

1. Staying true to yourself.
2. Considering the value of announcing your view...is it for sharing, growing, or learning, or is it just for shock value or to "be talking".
3. Knowing your audience.
4. Deciding if what you said were a headline with your name and photo on the front page of every newspaper and website, would you still say it.
5. Being prepared to accept the consequences of your actions/ideas/words (good or bad).

If all those are in check, then you will likely not be surprised by the responses or find yourself backpedaling from your words later.

LUNDBERGism

Your actions are a reflection of your attitude, and your attitude guides your actions. Where one ends and the other begins is not relevant, as they are intertwined.

Section 2:

Professional Behaviors

"Good manners sometimes means simply putting up with other people's bad manners." ~ H. Jackson Brown, Jr.

Professional behaviors may include types of communication and approaches, and even border on ways to have thriving relationships. Still, at the root of the following section on professional behaviors, there are actions involved with intent as the driver, and results in the end. Being professional is a combination of awareness, courtesy, opportunity, and even forgiveness and perspective. These behaviors may seem like a lesson in manners or etiquette, and in some ways, they are…regardless of the label you give them, they encourage consideration of others for the betterment of the situation.

Chapter 22
Invest in You

"The greatest works are done by the ones. The hundreds do not often do much, the companies never; it is the units, the single individuals, that are the power and the might." ~ Philemon Charles H. Spurgeon

Whether you make a little or a lot, you have *you*, your talent, your success, and your future, to look toward, anticipate, and create. In order to lean on that vision of what you will be ensure you look to find ways, to educate, to support, and to invest in just that...you!

At any point in your life or career (the sooner the better, and no time is too late), decide you are going to invest in you and your development.

You are encouraged to pick a percentage instead of a dollar amount, so that as your income changes (likely grows, but may shrink for life reasons and choices of yours and others), you will be consistent in your contribution to your future.

Your funds may go toward classes, books, on-line learning, coaching, support or other things you deem as something that will improve you either at that time, or in the future for the direction in which you are going.

Once you invest in yourself year over year, you will not see it as an expense, or even a cost of doing business, rather you will embrace it and even look forward to making that investment.

LUNDBERGism

Ensure you are focused on your self-worth before you even consider focusing on your net worth!

Chapter 23
Mobile Device Etiquette - Oxymoronic? Not Necessarily...

"Whoever one is, and wherever one is, one is always in the wrong if one is rude." ~ *Maurice Baring*

Sadly, when there is technology that assists us, there is technology that annoys us. If something can enhance, it also can repel. In the case of cellular phones or mobile devices, though, it is less the technology or enhancements that get us going...it is the people operating them who have the opportunity to follow sound guidelines or just blatantly show disregard for everyone but themselves!

The phrase "mobile device etiquette" need not be the latest in Oxymorons (something that counters itself by the definitions of the words/descriptions like "Jumbo Shrimp").

There are only a few appropriate places to talk on your mobile device, including (and surely not limited to, but to start...

1. In your office.

2. In your home.

3. In your car (preferably on a hands-free device or consider parking your car due the distraction of talking and driving and the possibility of a liability issue).

4. On a park bench where nobody else is relaxing.

5. In your yard.

6. In places where people will not be interrupted, disturbed, or distracted.

All of these places are at a low level, briefly (okay, your home may be an exception...especially since few people keep land-lines with long distance service any more) and in an "indoor voice"!

What is an indoor voice? Remember when you were a child? You could yell and scream outside and as soon as you were indoors, your volume when from 10 to 1-2 or you knew you were getting a time out or worse? The same is true for mobile device usage...only we don't have anyone giving time outs...wouldn't that be great? For an unknown, and surely perplexing reason, people tend to raise their voices while on their phones. Seriously, it's been a long time since a phone's microphone could not carry your voice...your mouth is on top of the microphone, so if someone "can't hear you now", get a new phone, new location, or new friend!

Remember, there are insecure attention hogs in our world who actually think they are cooler when they talk loudly on purpose to "show off". For them, any attention is good attention and a "shhhhhh" is like cheering them on and encouraging their behavior. Give them no attention, no looks, no energy other than simply giving them this tip, smiling and just walking away! Interestingly, though, there are so many places not to talk on your mobile device and among the most offensive (and not surprisingly, the list is longer than appropriate places) are:

1. The stall of a restroom (come on - nobody is that important that she or he is in demand even on the toilet...not to mention the disregard for the person on the on the other end of the phone...flushing is the least of the offensives!).

   <Slobification Snippet>
   While in the midst of edits of this book, I was traveling to/from California to meet with clients and deliver a training and a speaking engagement. It was a Sunday afternoon when I landed in Denver only to find my quick stop in the restroom not only overshadowed by someone on the phone in a stall, she was on the phone in a stall on speaker phone! Just when I thought the world could not be more Slobified, she quickly proved me wrong!

2. At airport gates (sure, you are likely there for 45+ minutes, and with a bunch of people you don't know, so what makes talking on your phone - usually loudly, and with the same details over and over, something to do then?) If you want to use your phone, stand up and walk around while keeping your voice at the "indoor voice" level and without telling everyone "I'm at the airport - yeah, in Boston".

3. In elevators (seriously...poor reception, enclosed space and a lot of stops...did you really think that would work?).

4. In line with other people, in particular when you reach the checkout/bank teller/attendant. (These

are people too, and how would you like it if during your job people consistently ignored you and talked to others? Give them the respect they deserve and perhaps they will treat the rest of us kindly).

5. At sporting events (I get it, you want people to know you are there...OK, but during the plays you are standing and yelling...sit down and enjoy the game)! Okay, if you want to talk while seated and before the game or in between plays or at half-time, we'll excuse it, but not standing at or on your chair and yelling! This is just like being at the movies or during a play. Make a choice...it's called "opportunity cost" either you are at the event or on the phone...not both! Note: even the light emitted while texting during a movie or play is blindly offensive to others...especially those behind you.

6. At dinner with other people (are the people you are with not good enough?). This is typically when I just leave. Give that a whirl...leave when someone else takes a call at lunch or dinner with you. When they ask you about it, just tell them you value your time and want to spend it focused...not ignored or taken for granted. Oh, and take off your flashing blue tooth when you are at dinner...you just look silly with your family or spouse...how can they take you seriously when you look like you'll soon be "beamed up"?

7. On trains or buses (still confined spaces...let's hope we do not get the ability to talk on phones on planes...it'll be like a human circus on altitude without well-circulated air...I see

issues!!) or even in a car with someone else driving or any other passengers.

8. At your doctor's office (nobody needs, and rarely anyone wants, to hear how drunk you were last night, or the reason you are at the doctor - other than the nurses and doctors). Spare us, have some dignity and self-respect, please!

9. During a business meeting or a speaker's presentation (if you have ever been in one of my public or private speaking engagements, if a mobile device rings, I say "Oh, if that is for me, please tell them I am far too busy to take that right now" just for emphasis).

10. At weddings and/or funerals (if you need an explanation here, you're likely not going to take kindly to these tips anyway, so "no comment").

Mobile device etiquette also includes a time management component. Consider the real "need" or opportunity cost to take or make a call in the company of others. Unless you are expecting an urgent call (and you would set this expectation with others upon your encounter) your time, focus, and interactions with those around you are not only appreciated, but also an indication of respect or lack thereof. It is also disrespectful to the person you are calling or taking their call if you are not able to provide them with your undivided attention. Voicemail is much more respectful and considerate to the person calling you if you cannot give them your undivided attention. There is nothing more ridiculous than answering your mobile device just to say "I can't talk right now." Use a little smart planning/time management before placing a cell phone call. Open your eyes, look around, and think ahead. Are you about to enter into an area where cellular calls are commonly dropped (elevators, parking garages, etc.) or the background noise will be too loud (near heavy traffic or high blowing wind)? A little time and situation awareness and ownership will waste less of your time and/or that of the other person on the call.

Also, a ring tone is humorous or entertaining perhaps once, twice or a third time, but not ever at work or in a business setting. After it has worn out its welcome, buy a new ring tone, put your phone on vibrate or silent, or heck, just use one of the handfuls of generic ring tones (like on old-school phones). Rudy Giuliani made a great move which was wonderful for New York City when he minimized car horn abuse, and now we can do that for mobile devices by keeping a smile on our face, committing to the appropriate places and resisting the "chatter" in the inappropriate locations! So, let's leave the oxymoron comments to be "Old News".

Chapter 24
PEG(G) Your Excess and Gain Control!

"One cannot manage too many
affairs: like pumpkins in the water,
one pops up while you try to hold
down the other." ~ *Chinese Proverb*

Interestingly enough, whether it is a holiday season, time of celebration, time of reflection, time of consideration, or the time of one's life, excess in the form of

Personal spending,
Eating,
Gifts and **G**uilt

tend to be prevalent.

In order to avoid such tendencies, please consider the following guidelines:

With personal spending, remember that every activity, party or event does not require the complete detailing of your car, a new outfit, some fine jewelry, etc. Allow your personal spending to be one or two gifts to you from you at this time. Remember that the reason you were included in the invitations to the parties is because of who you are, rather than what you wear or have. Resist saying "I can't afford that" or "My wife would kill me if she knew I bought that". Phrase things internally and externally to reflect a positive positioning such as, "That does not suit my financial plan right now," or "I'd like to discuss the best approach with my wife before moving forward," when faced with the buying/spending pressure (even if it is self-induced!) so that you are in a positive state of mind when making purchases.

As far as eating goes, it seems easier at festivities to resist resisting! When at parties or events, consider eating a healthy, light, well-balanced meal prior to arriving so that you are not famished when you get to the location. People often think they will not eat a thing all day because they are going to overindulge later, but that makes most people cranky and likely to gorge. The way to keep eating in check is to allow, yes, grant permission to yourself to once or twice a week have dessert, or to have a handful of candy or nuts (that's one handful – not a baseball glove full!), and let it be. What we do not tend to go to excess in around holidays and celebrations, is exercise (see January 5th – 25th for that!), so if you decide you are going to have some extra fat grams and/or calories, plan to work out for an additional 15 minutes to 30 minutes in order to counter the effects. Resist saying "Oh I have gained so much weight, why not?" or "It's a time to celebrate, of course we are all eating" or "I am on a diet". These statements take the control away from you, where expressions/responses such as "No thank you, that looks lovely, though", or "Yes, thanks, a small piece is perfect", or "Thank you, I am just full right now", will be polite, not draw attention to your weight or diet, and allow you to stay in conversation about something other than diets and waistlines.

Gift-giving and what to whom, when and how much is something of a challenge, too, right? Well, in planning your gifts, first have a plan. While it may be momentarily fun to just go out and start spending, much like personal spending, gift-giving can create financial concerns later when not thought through early in the holiday season. Consider a good fit for your financial plan after recording all the people for whom you want to give a gift. Make a list, and stick to it. For people who are new in your life or you are unsure about a gift, have a conversation with them by suggesting you have lunch as your gift to each other or get a group together to have an ornament exchange so there is not silly gift-giving just to be participating, and the discussion takes place prior to purchases being made. Resist showering people with lavish things that will make you feel good for the time being…until you get your credit card bill. You may even want to get out cash for holiday shopping so that you actually see and feel the impact of each purchase and enjoy the fact you are working your financial plan while being thoughtful and considerate as a gift-giver.

Guilt is last in the list since it can stem from any of the earlier mentioned activities. It also stems from the interactions, or lack there of, with friends and family at holidays, celebrations, losses, school events or gatherings. Watch being a victim of guilt as well as being a giver of guilt. Embrace things like setting aside time on the phone with no multi-tasking as part of spending time with your aunt or grandfather if you cannot be together. If/when someone states you "really should be here for the holidays" respond (not react) with "It's wonderful you extend such a generous invitation, and I appreciate that you respect my decision to stay home", or "It's wonderful to be so loved, let's enjoy the time we do have together now on the phone and share photos with each other afterward." Resist reacting with, "I know, but I just can't right now" or "Yes, but I can't afford it" or "You just don't understand." These comments make you defensive, and you are much better off to stay focused and appreciative. The other temptation with guilt is to ignore some of these suggestions and then feel badly about that. If you do overspend, overeat or just overindulge in gifts, decide if you are going to accept that and

1. Move on, or
2. Make returns, or
3. Make a plan.

Whichever is selected should be embraced and not revisited. Reliving and reassessing just makes guilty feelings increase. Progress, not perfection is what we are striving to attain, so know that not all things will go smoothly, and look for ways to decrease the bumps without making yourself feel awful for changing things this year.

While using each of the mentioned suggestions, remember that no excuses are needed. People do not want to hear the back story…that is just taking more of their time and attention…rather, just smile, state what you want and keep direct, friendly, and positive! With these ideas in mind, make it a focused, intentional, and enjoyable time, and life, for you!

Chapter 25
Timing is Telling

"People count up the faults of those who keep them waiting." ~ French Proverb

In our society of fast, busy, go, go, go, with cellular phones and wireless everything, it seems like there would be no miscommunication regarding time...but there still is...often, and without much thought for the person waiting.

The time to let someone know you are behind schedule, running late, or stopping to do something before seeing him or her, is long before the scheduled time.

Let's say that you have a 1:30 PM meeting ½ hour away from your home or office, and it is currently 1:10 PM. Here are your choices:

A) Hop in the car and crank the tunes...what is a few minutes anyway?
B) Start thinking of excuses!
C) Touch up your hair and check your clothes because if you're going to be tardy, you might as well look fabulous upon entry.
D) Get in the car and start driving really fast...maybe you can make it!
E) Contact the person with whom you are meeting or the office where you are expected immediately, and ask him or her to:

1) Please forgive you.
2) Simply state you miscalculated and are 10 minutes behind.
3) Ask if the meeting can please still take place.

Hopefully you chose E! With that smart choice, reflect on what you usually do…is the answer still E? Part of the answer in E is that you do not make excuses or provide your history, your "back story". This other person should not have to listen to that while rearranging something and/or accommodating you.

The primary reason for acting on choice E is that it shows courtesy toward the other person. Perhaps that individual or office can get something else done in those 10 minutes. An errand can be run, a note written, a story read, etc., and with that warning, so to speak, the other person has the option about his or her time…without that warning, you are basically proving that you think your time is more valuable than the other person.

Another reason for following through on E is that you are calm and focused and less likely to make frantic driving decisions or cause situations for others on your path.

Timing is not everything, but surely timing is tremendously telling with respect to availability, and in this case, disposition and respect, so remember that next time you are running late…and act on the knowledge that the E answer provides you not with an excuse but rather ownership of your actions.

Chapter 26
Be Willing and Able to COACH

"A man can be as great as he wants to be. If you believe in yourself and have the courage, the determination, the dedication, the competitive drive and if you are willing to sacrifice the little things in life and pay the price for the things that are worthwhile, it can be done."
~ *Vince Lombardi*

Coaching is not just something that takes place on a field, or in a partnership like I have with my valued clients, rather being a coach is a skill that is demonstrated best with a process and approach that is consistent...whether coaching to change behavior, to ensure repeat performance, or even for an accolade.

A guideline I have developed and share in workshops and one-on-one, is that of COACH. Quite directly, COACH stands for:

Connect
Ownership
Assessment
Collaboration
Have a plan

In the *Connect* portion, strive to make a personal interaction with a sincere energy and genuine question, if you chose to ask one. *Ownership* comes from accountability on both parts...yours and the other person's. *Assessment* is that of the intake of the situation or result for reviewing and focusing forward. *Collaboration* means what part you will handle (if any) and what agreement you are in with the other person. *Have* a plan comes from the one being coached...not you...allow and even insist on the coachee devising a plan.

Let's imagine a coaching with a child, student or team member where there is a problem with the result:

Connect with a meeting and an agenda (even if it is just verbal) and ask how the person thought the report/meeting/interaction went...then, listen fully. *Ownership* follows when each party becomes accountable by stating what he/she did to get the result. *Assessment* is the exploration of how things could have gone more smoothly. *Collaboration* is reaching agreement after sharing ideas on what to do differently. *Have* a plan is the child, student, or team member relaying what he/she specifically learned and will do moving forward.

Now, let's move to the desire to have behaviors/performance/results repeated:

Connect with a meeting and an agenda (even if it is just verbal) and ask how the person thought the report/meeting/interaction went...then, listen fully. *Ownership* follows when each party becomes accountable by stating what he/she did to get the result. *Assessment* is the exploration of how things did not go wrong and what kept them on track. *Collaboration* is reaching agreement after sharing ideas on what to do in similar and different situations to yield the same results. *Have* a plan is the child, student, or team member relaying what he/she specifically was recognized for doing correctly and assuring that a similar fashion will be habit to yield the appropriate results.

Finally, it is imperative we coach when providing praise and recognition! Please picture and engage in the COACH approach when sharing an accolade:

Connect with a meeting and an agenda (even if it is just verbal) and ask how the person thought the report/meeting/interaction went. Then, listen fully. *Ownership* follows when each party becomes accountable by stating what he/she did to get the result. *Assessment* is the exploration of how things went well and giving credit to that person for his/her ideas/efforts/results. *Collaboration* is reaching agreement after sharing ideas on what to do to maintain that level of effort and even ask for ideas on how to do it yourself. *Have* a plan is the child, student or team member relaying what he/she specifically heard from you and any other ideas based on the sincere praise.

While we would all like to be in the latter of the situations often, the more we recognize those times to offer appreciation, the less likely we will be in the first category with the same people over and over. The COACHing tool is invaluable, and is best used when used in concert with consistently including open ended questions and sincere listening to the questions posed.

Knowing all of these things, keep in mind that while you may not have a clipboard in your hand and/or hat on your head, you have the tools to be a great COACH!

LUNDBERGism

A win is not a real *win* when it comes at too big of a cost, and a loss is not a true *loss* when advancement is made.

Chapter 27
Process: How is it Done...And What Can You Do With It?

"Life is a process of becoming, a combination of states we have to go through. Where people fail is that they wish to elect a state and remain in it. This is a kind of death." ~ *Anais Nin*

If you have ever wondered what people do differently to handle the same information, knowing how you process data, situations, and even basic input, is useful in gaining insight into others' perspective as well. There is a way each of us is wired, and based on that internal wiring, we are somewhat predictable in our positioning, statements, and/or emotions after certain occurrences or predicaments.

Consider this, people function in one of four ways when given input, they *Process and React, Process and Protect, Process and Question,* or *Process and Respond.*

Process and React is when someone hears, sees, smells, and/or feels something and simply acts on that experience. He/she is reacting and there is more a sense of urgency and drive than accuracy and thought to the effect. This person is often hasty, overlooking a possibility that would have taken just slight exploration. *Process and React* individuals tend to measure once and cut two or three times.

Process and Protect is when someone hears, sees, smells, and/or feels something and immediately knows what works best for him/her and yet they say nothing. He/she is protecting either the person with whom he/she is interacting (not likely) or him/herself. This person does not want to be wrong and can even go to the extreme of not sharing a good, sound answer/idea for fear of being criticized or because he/she wants to be the "I told you so" or hero in the end. *Process and Protect* individuals measure once or more, always in private, and wait to cut until their cut is needed, requested or required.

Process and Question is when someone hears, sees, smells, and/or feels something and immediately voices the need for further information/experience. This is the "question bug" of sorts who can be either realistic or pessimistic depending on how he/she thinks/operates. The *Process and Question* person acts out of a need to know and have things "resolved" and can be perceived (or actually be) negative when the questions consistently show themselves as doubt. *Process and Question* people tend to measure at least twice and ask you if to cut, or minimally when to cut. And if they cut, they kindly and readily suggest you to always do it the way he/she did.

Process and Respond happens when someone hears, sees, smells, and/or feels something and calmly considers options so quickly and reasonably that it appears to be a reaction, when in fact there is no sense of urgency, rather sensibility and sharing of what he/she thinks is "common sense". He/she is fast with the logical removal of ill-fated ideas and considers him or herself not all-knowing, rather grounded. The *Process and Respond* people measure twice and cut once...and it seems effortless.

What is suggested you do about this awareness? Please keep in mind first, how you are wired...be honest...are you a *Reactor,* a *Questioner,* a *Protector*, or a *Responder*? None are bad or wrong, rather, as you move down from 1 to 4, you (hopefully) see the more admired/appreciated versions of how people process things. You can change your processing, regardless of your natural "wiring". If you tend to *Process and React*, you would serve yourself well to ask yourself what is a good response before acting. If you likely *Process and Protect*, try to let go of judgment and think of the greater good rather than just you and the impact on you. When you are a *Process and Question* person, imagine sharing, rather than telling, after you get the answers to the questions, and think through the questions before asking so many it makes someone anxious. If you *Process and Respond*, please remember not all of us are as calm and logical and what is "common sense" to you may be neither common nor sensible to others.

Likewise, when interacting with others, you can have greater success with partnering when you leverage the type for that person (and you). If a person is typically a *Process and React* individual, give details first, lead up to the information with a story and options so the person does not over-react.

When interacting with a *Process and Protect* person, show vulnerability where it is and verbalize the want/need for his/her input and ideas in order to allow for ease of sharing. At times when you are working with a *Process and Question* person, allow patience to be your guide…asking if you are clear and for more questions rather than impatiently asking "does that make sense?". And, with the *Process and Respond* people, share your admiration and ask them to verbalize or document any of the fleeting considerations they calmly and quickly discerned would not fit in order to model them and learn from them.

Knowing how you *Process* will assist you in interacting, and being aware of others' approaches will enlighten you as well…bringing you both closer to an agreeable way to decide on things/direction/options when working toward agreed-upon, workable goals.

<u>LUNDBERGism</u>

If perception is reality, keep in mind it is the other person's perception that often impacts *your* reality!

Chapter 28
Sporting Event Etiquette

"Sporting goods companies pay me not to endorse their products." ~ Bob Uecker

It's a big day…you have your tickets, you are ready to cheer with your friends or family, or minimally other fans, and there it is…rudeness that is so incomprehensible, it actually takes away from the touchdown visions, the home run hopes, the goal scoring anticipation…the whole nine yards, so to speak!

How do you avoid being one of those fans? First, remember that the word fan stems from the less popular and clearly more negative word, fanatic. Second, follow these simple rules for behaving beautifully while at a sporting event:

1. When in America (sporting event or not) walk to your right…walk like you drive and that goes for getting to the level your seats are on, finding your seat and exiting your seat. There are typically two sides to the stairs at venues. Stick to your right, and you will have the right of way. This will avoid the awkward (no, it is not endearing or cute) "dance" in the aisle with another fan.

2. When you arrive at your aisle, if your seat is not on the end, smile at the people in the seats between you and your seats, and say "excuse me, please". Stating things like "I'm there", or

"I need to get through" shows ignorance, inconsideration, and a lack of any manners whatsoever. Hopping over seats to avoid the excuse me's is not recommended either.

3. Be silent during the national anthem if you are not going to sing it. Yes, men, take off your hats, and ladies, you do not need to remove yours.

4. Be silent during moments of silence or prayers. Even if you do not pray or believe in what is being observed, a time for lame protests in the form of talking makes for distraction and for showing you are completely uncouth.

5. Since you will likely get up during a game, match or round, please do so in-between activities, plays, etc. Standing during the middle of a run is great if you are cheering and everyone is doing the same. Standing during a critical face off just to disrupt everyone so you can grab a beer or powder your nose, is not acceptable. The same is true for returning to your seat…do it between the action-packed parts of the game. Your activity should not prohibit the fans' ability to view the teams' activity.

6. When someone else gets up to exit an aisle, avoid standing if possible, but if they are large or the seat rows are small, stand quickly and sit back down immediately. Better yet, instead of standing, turn your legs with your knees bent, in the direction the other person is heading. This allows for smooth pass through and no bumping of bodies.

7. If you do not know the game, attempt to read up on it prior to the activities commencing. If you have a question, ask between plays.

8. Keep your phone low or off. You are out at an event…isn't that enough for you? If you have it on for a possible emergency or your sitter, keep it on low, and when you take the call, speak low and down with your hand covering your mouth. Most of us attending the event do not want to hear your conversation!

9. If you are meeting someone at the event, make your plan something more thoughtful and creative than both being in your seats during the game calling one another and standing and waving to "find" each other.

10. Do not talk on your mobile phone while in a stall in the restroom. While I am at it, this goes for any restroom…a bar, a restaurant, a book store, a library…I have seen, or rather, heard them all…and they are the epitome of over-indulged, over-inflated self-important-ness. Get over yourself and go cheer like a good fan!!

Let it be a big day…you have your tickets, you are ready to cheer with your friends or family, or other fans, so make it a most enjoyable, and memorable (for all the well-serving and kind reasons) sporting event!

Chapter 29
Some Things Cost Little, and Offer So Much...

"The obstacles you face are...
mental barriers which can be broken
by adopting a more positive
approach." ~ *Clarence Blasier*

Want to make someone's day and potentially make yours, too? Is there somebody you want to meet? Are you ever in a meeting/group where you could outreach? Do you sometimes ignore your own thoughts of interacting? Of course...and since we are going for progress not perfection with all my coaching tips to grow you, I encourage you to see the opportunity to make a connection, think of something or some place you like/enjoy (for peace and calm), take a breath, smile, put your shoulders back, make eye contact, and extend your right hand with a firm handshake, continue your smile and look the other person squarely in the eye as you introduce yourself by name slowly and loudly.

You will likely be surprised what this welcoming, confident approach will accomplish for you and the other person, too. If the recipient of your extended hand is shocked or does not react, make him/her feel included, by simply asking "and your name is?"

Start positive and you will typically be encouraged by what can happen. So few people do such and you will be surprised how well it works. In the real world, where we all live and learn, smiles, handshakes, approaches and, eventually, the overall and underlying environment, all count. We do create our environment and by showing a friendly, thoughtful approach and allowing others to feel comfortable, we make the situation enjoyable, or minimally bearable...and it has the chance to grow from there.

<Slobification Snippet>
While at a charity golf tournament, I saw someone I met at the prior year's tournament. My husband and I waved and went over to greet him. "Hello, I'm Debbie Lundberg," I said as we shook hands, and he responded, "I know!" A bit surprised, but not shocked, as people are Slobified after all, hoping to get him to state his name, next I said, "And, this is my husband, Michael Lundberg"; to which he replied "I remember you, too!" With two opportunities for him to share his name, he opted out, and there I was left to ask, "Please forgive me, with a year in between the last time we met, I am not recalling your name...and your name is, please?" He could have been kind, professional, and even just thoughtful when we shook hands and simply restated his name!

So, the next time you see someone of interest, get out of your center, focus on that person, recall something or someone you find pleasant (as an emotional reference), take a breath, smile, stand tall, make eye contact, and extend your right hand with a firm handshake through your smile and direct gaze as you introduce yourself by name slowly and proudly...that person may just be your next client, friend, soulmate, or confidant...and if you don't take the first step, you'll never know. Remember, this effort costs you so little, and yet the return on the investment has endless possibilities.

Chapter 30
Adopt and Adapt

"Adapt or perish, now as ever, is nature's inexorable imperative."
~ *H. G. Wells*

Often it has been said and heard that imitation is the most sincere form of flattery...it is even a proverb, yet few of us feel quite that way when someone presents what looks like our work, or appears in the same outfit/suit we have on that day. Often flattery feels like trickery or something not well thought through.

What gives?

Perhaps Benjamin Franklin said it best when he announced, "There is much difference between imitating a man and counterfeiting him." I happen to agree with the beloved Mr. Franklin, and I suggest the concept of adopt and adapt.

Adopt and adapt is when you see, hear, feel, or experience something another person does or says or believes and you consider it, process it, perhaps research it further, and configure it to your situation or style. In other words, first you observe, second, you experience, third, you incorporate, and fourth, you present. I like the fact that Dr. Joyce Brothers said, "Listening, not imitation, may be the sincerest form of flattery" because for me, it is part of that first step of observation. Observation happens fully when all senses are engaged. As simple as a new fashion trend is, if we partake in it, it is about the look, feel, response, happiness, etc…and that may be just a skinny jean, or wide belt! Imagine what will take place when you are looking at styles, impact, approaches, or philosophies!

How do you give credit where credit is due?

"No one ever became great by imitation" according to Samuel Johnson! So how are we great when the world is not spinning off its axis with truly original ideas? It is that we give credit 100% for direct quotations, full processes, or uses of materials such as articles or books, and we give partial credit for conceptual ideas or summations that are tempered with personal opinion. The reference is for respect and referral for the person first learning of an idea. At no time do we effectively just "borrow" or outright steal ideas, concepts, etc. Still, we have the right to base our opinions/actions on others…it would be difficult not to do so.

Simply put, if we are leaning toward someone's fashion style, or directly copying it, at the least, let the person know that he/she inspired you, that they may see a bit of their style in yours and that you appreciate their leading the way and/or introducing you to that look/feel. With work style and efforts, do the same by using expressions like "You stated that well…I am making a note of that" or "Thank you for the insight, I will be incorporating that in my next presentation".

What you do not want to do, is watch every gesture, move and nuance and attempt to replicate it…fashion-wise or work-style-wise. Most of us have undoubtedly seen the student attempt to become the teacher by literally masquerading as the teacher. It is not only awkward, but embarrassing for those of us experiencing it right along with the person demonstrating it!

You'll be a second rate someone-else-imitator, and you have the ability to consistently be a first-rate you. Keep that in mind, and adopt what you like about an idea/presentation/style. Adapt it to you, and you will continue to be unique and evolving. According to Mahatma Gandhi, "Adaptability is not imitation. It means power of resistance and assimilation". I believe you are adaptable, and there is no need for thoughtless or shallow flattery here!

LUNDBERGism

Care less about your impression(s) on those who are careless in their impressions of you.

Chapter 31
To Give or Not to Give...

"The greatest gift you can give another is the purity of your attention." ~ *Richard Moss*

With holiday seasons and birthdays/anniversaries regularly in full bloom, there is often the question of what for whom and simply whom to include. Here's a suggestion: if you are thinking you *should* give, do not give and if you *want* to give, then do give. Callous? No, rather, it is honest. Some people give to get and others give to impress, but that is not the true spirit of a gift. Please remember that giving and gifts are just that...from one to another without obligation, guilt, or score-keeping.

So, for those whom you respect, admire, appreciate, love, adore, like so much it feels great or just want to express gratitude, go on out (or stay in and on-line) and shop or make something or write a card or print a photo to frame. For those who you sense competition, distrust, unworthiness or judgment, think kind thoughts and wish them well and hope for a better relationship...better yet, work on how you can/will interact most effectively or without anger or competition back and let such growth be your gift to you and them.

This idea may have you wondering what to do, though, if someone gives you a gift and you have none in return. It's simple - smile and say "Thank you"...period. Please refrain from making an excuse that their gift is on order or at home or you are still shopping. Recall the earlier message on gifts and be appreciative without a sense of obligatory reciprocity. If in fact you are still shopping or it is at home, just arrange to send it or deliver it yourself. An excuse minimizes their effort and focuses back on you...let the giver enjoy the pleasures of giving. If you like, based on the relationship, and not only the gift, the next time you are together, pay for lunch or coffee or pick up something when you see what seems a fit...even if it is long past the holidays.

If all of us will keep in mind that communication is at the heart of everything, we'd ask those around us if they want to exchange gifts or share time or get lunch, so really, most of the awkwardness can and will be avoided by broaching the subject earlier rather than later. Still, if that has not been done, and you want to give, go right on giving and if you get something from someone, go ahead and say thanks and lose the internal/mental scorecard and let it be a joy rather than anything close to a burden.

LUNDBERGism

Mind the Gap between your expectations and your approach, and see the difference *in* you...as well as the difference *for* those following you.

Chapter 32
Re-engaged Commitment in Just Four Steps

"Unless commitment is made, there are only promises and hopes; but no plans." ~ Peter F. Drucker

People check out. People get distracted. Each of us is part of that group called "people". If you are seeing challenges in people being committed fully to school, the family, work, or the team, consider these four steps (in order) to re-engage and get results:

1. Take time to look back. Allowing people to briefly discuss the good and the bad of the past year (rather than the "bury your head in the sand about the economy" approach far too many are taking...or worse yet, the "sky is falling", let's complain, complain, complain approach) will make it known that you are aware, that you care, and that you are willing to listen and share.

2. Project long and short-term results. The long term, big picture, will keep things in mind, and the weekly or bi-weekly goals will allow perspective, accomplishment and a sense of reward for efforts made.

3. Get the input from all. When your family or your team is going forward with a trip or a project, they may not be the decision makers, but you can sincerely find a way to allow their input to matter and be seen in the end. Consider asking for a theme idea for a trip with the family

and ask colleagues and team members at work
for the pros and cons...the potential pitfalls and
winner circle moments. Make sure you listen
and learn, as you are likely to hear something
you have not considered.

4. Reflect on the day/week/month/quarter with
   what went well and what can/will be improved.
   Celebrate successes and head off potential
   disasters with open communication and
   planning.

Through taking time to look back, projecting long-
term and short-term results, getting input from all
involved, and reflecting on the time frames
consistently, you will get re-engagement and
productive, communicative family, team, or group
members throughout the year!

LUNDBERGism

A conversation is not a commitment...ensure you
have a commitment before expecting something
to happen based on what just may be something
the other person views as a lighthearted chat...

Chapter 33
"Triple A" Social Media for B2B & B2C

"Don't say anything online that you wouldn't want plastered on a billboard with your face on it." ~ Erin Bury

For "Triple A" engagement and outcomes for your social media efforts in the realm of Business-to-Business (B2B) and Business to Consumer (B2C), consider the following A's:

ASSIST. Think in terms of assisting your followers, readers, subscribers, and onlookers. How are you a resource to offer ideas, people, and other resources. This is not the realm to sell, sell, sell! This is the area to offer, show, share, and connect. The business will follow where appropriate. Be seen as the expert who offers freely without expectation, and when the time is right, others will engage in your services and/or products.

ACT. Interface with others on the sites and media you use (LinkedIn, Facebook, Names, Blogs, Twitter, Plaxo, etc.). Take action by posting, commenting, and sharing where appropriate. Resist being a know-it-all, rather share questions or thoughts like "have you considered XYZ?" so that you are acting in their interest by sharing your information/ideas.

APPRECIATE. Show thanks to those who assist you, act on your posts and/or offer criticism or other ideas for your approach and/or your business. Even a bad review is welcomed, as it gives you free feedback that you can address and might not have known before. No matter what is posted, thank the person for the idea, taking the time, etc. Appreciation shows you care and does not present you in a defensive way.

If you are unsure about Social Media, jump in, have fun, and remember, it is one aspect of your business approach and marketing, so commit to it, do it minimally twice a week, be consistent in your approach, and enjoy the opportunities...and the learning!

Chapter 34
Of the ABCs, Focus on the HIJ...

"We come nearest to the great when we are great in humility."
~ Rabindranath Tagore

When asked recently by a client "what is the true secret to success?" I replied that there is no secret to success...rather the funny thing about personal and professional success is that both are related...and both are attainable by following the ABCs, or at least the HIJs: Humility, Interest, and Joy!

Humility. The first thing anyone who is successful (truly successful, not just wealthy in terms of his or her financials) knows, is while "it ain't braggin' if it's true." humility goes much farther with people than continuous claims of feats.

<Slobification Snippet>
I believe we all know the "Toppers" - you'll recall them...the men or women who have a story for everything...and it tops whoever preceded them. For example, if you bowled a 237, he/she bowled a 260, and if you sat on the 40-yard line at the Super Bowl, somehow that person was nearer the 50-yard line, and of course, if you climbed Mt. Everest, the Topper, scaled it in 30 degree below zero weather...likely in a Speedo!

These Toppers are memorable and forgotten all at once. They are remembered for all the wrong reasons and their true talent (and they likely have some) is lost in translation. Humility, on the other hand, is the ability and belief that learning can be found everywhere and from most everyone. The humble person looks at the opportunities to network, participate, lead, follow, etc. in the same way...by anticipating growth and lessons...and eagerly welcomes them.

Interest. While the humble one is interesting because of that trait, his or her being interested is a complement to his/her humility. Being *interesting* sadly far exceeds being *interested* in the way a lot of people act. *But, it is the kind and remembered, often revered person, who is genuinely interested over attempting to be interesting!* Think this is not true? I adapted this from a lovely woman from NY who now lives in FL...enter a party/event/meeting and look at the number of people in the room and divide that number into the number of minutes you will be there, THAT is the amount of time you have to be interesting...the rest of the time is demonstrating, and therefore, learning from, your interest in others. Rarely does a person share tales the entire day or night and be thought of as a caring or genuine person...maybe a fun, adventuresome or loud soul, but rarely the person someone engages in continued conversation, sharing and work or personal opportunities. If this is a challenge for you, just remember to ask yourself, am I listening more than I am speaking? If so, then I am likely demonstrating my being interested. If I am speaking more than I am listening, then I am either the honored guest or presenter, or I am feebly grasping at being interesting. If I am neither listening nor talking aloud a lot, I must be talking to myself...and that is an entirely different topic!!

Joy. Finally, in this alphabet soup chapter, there is success in simply sharing the joy with others. When someone else has success or good fortune, be entirely happy for and with that person to welcome his/her news with joy. It is the joyous friend or acquaintance who is contacted and included since jealousy, envy, and disappointment are not consuming that friend. Someone who can and does truly offer joy and happiness to others is one who is giving of self and learning of self and others. Where there is joy for another, there will be joy for that person. In the big picture, the joy that is experienced with and for the news regarding individuals or teams who have accomplished their goals or come into money, fame, or any form of desired recognition, is a reflection of one's own self confidence, experience and appreciation for life. Who is not encouraged by and attracted to another who is joyous? Only the person who is negative, unforgiving, or undisciplined...so not only is joy a measure of self-assuredness, but a gauge for sincerity and reliability in a friend or colleague.

As you think about the things you aspire to do, be, or have, please go back or stay back, at the basics of the ABC's of the HIJ. If you are finding one or more of the HIJ principles taxing, please consider the reflection of what it is you are accomplishing. Without the humility, you are being boastful, and none of us is perfect. What will happen when you err? You get what you give and there will not be much forgiveness readily available had you been thoughtless in your responses. Should self-interest supersede your interest in others, you might be lonely or insecure. Again, each of us has things for which we seek improvement. Go forward to improve rather than mask it. The interest in others gains awareness and impact...and friends and colleagues alike. It is tough to be lonely or insecure when you share interests and a basis for friendship and success together. When the joy is gone, find it in knowing that your turn is out there and with focus, support and direction, you will be receiving joy for your goals too...maybe, not just right then. Take from the accomplishments of others and incorporate style or approach to make it your own. There is joy in learning, doing and experiencing.

While the tip may be as simple as three letters, three words, three concepts; the success comes in finding those things… the humility, interest, and joy, within you and conveying that first and for yourself and secondly with others...and watch the way more of the same follows.

LUNDBERGism

Practice what you promote!
(No *preaching* required!)

Chapter 35
Manage These So You Can Lead Yourself and Others

"A leader is one who knows the way, goes the way, and shows the way."
~ John C. Maxwell

Often people ask, "How can I be good at managing others?" My reply is consistently the same one; "You don't manage people, you manage process; you lead people."

Having believed that and having said that repeatedly, there is one part of leading that involves the process of being human, and in striving to show leadership, please remember to first manage the following within you, for your ultimate leadership capability:

Your **ego and attitude**...there is no room for ego in leadership and egos get checked at the door when working with others.

Your **words**...spoken and written.

Your **motivation and approach**...being driven for others to be successful and the success of an entity or product versus money is longer lived...remember, humility subtly speaks volumes.

Your **personal life**...while popular or well-known people may be remembered, true leaders demonstrate balance.

Your **appreciation**...there can never be enough sincere, warranted appreciation.

Your **emotions**...emotional power does not mean hiding emotions, rather it means recognizing when and where emotions are appropriate to share.

Your **perspective**...while you may not agree with someone's position, consider that the history he/she has is different, and spend time respecting that.

Your **expectation** that capability + desire = results... since everyone's capability and/or desire may not be the same as yours; therefore, the results will not be either.

Your **brand**...that is what you and others can expect of you...and should.

When you manage these things, and address them in a mental checklist when engaging with others, you know that you are balanced and ready to interact, and therefore, in a position to lead others, rather than attempt to manage them!

Chapter 36
Parking Lot Protocol

"Treat everyone with politeness, even those who are rude to you - not because they are nice, but because you are." ~ *Unknown*

What is a tad disheartening is that a tip on parking lot protocol is greatly needed by many. Can you believe you are holding in your hands a book with a chapter entitled "Parking Lot Protocol"? I almost cannot, yet each time I am in a parking lot or ask others about their experiences in parking lots, the response of disgust, angst, and borderline fear arise.

Before we go too far, embrace the idea that no matter how small or fast your car, you are not cooler as a result of driving quickly, diagonally across a parking lot...no matter what you have previously believed! Parking lots are to serve parking needs, not those of egos or show-offs. Parking lots have speed limits of 10-20 miles per hour...and I think those are too high. Parking lots are places for parking and walking...with some very slow driving done to facilitate those two things.

It's true, I have nearly 200 skydives, have bungee jumped more than once, have been in a glider, hang-glided, ridden many a roller coaster, started my own business, spoken in front of hundreds of people, but one thing that gives me pause more than any of those, is when I get in a parking lot. It is as though people disregard the rules of driving, courtesy, and just plain sense!

Quickly and efficiently, here are the rules of the road for all of us:

1. Observe the speed limits.

2. Drive in aisles only in the direction that the vehicles are parked.

3. Know that crosswalks are just that; places for walkers to cross, not a sign to you to hurry up so the walkers wait for you!

4. Allow for pedestrians to cross. You are comfortable in a climate controlled vehicle, and they are not…let them pass. Signal with your hand (kindly) or your lights to indicate for them to go if they hesitate.

5. Park in the lines on the asphalt. The lines are not guidelines, they indicate spaces. If your car is too pristine or special to be in a space, leave it at home. Taking up more than one space invites people to squeeze in next to you and bang their door into yours anyway, so either park out far and walk, or get comfortable with being in the allowed space!

6. When you walk up to the building/facility where you are parked, if you spot a buggy out in the way, get it and either take it up to the store or put it in it's home called the cart corral. Sure, you did not leave it there, and you are not responsible for it, but be responsible in general and keep someone from having an issue with the

runaway cart getting in his or her way…or worse yet, it hitting someone's vehicle! The exception to this "rule" is a parent with children who require the parent to strap them in the car. After all, children are not to be left alone in a vehicle in the parking lot. The solution? Offer to return the cart for that parent so there are not stray carts left in the lot…all while keeping kids, cars, and drivers safe.

7. When walking (this is not all about driving), stay to your right. Much like in the Sporting Event Etiquette chapter, you need not question where to walk. The middle is never appropriate, and diagonally crossing is pure self-absorption!

8. Cross at crosswalks, and speed up your walking when a vehicle is awaiting your safe passage. Smile, wave and acknowledge the person in the vehicle who waited for you. (The same is true when a person in a vehicle lets you out into traffic when you are in your vehicle…it is commonly called "the courtesy wave").

Shop smart and well with these eight things…as they are quite effortless and easy. The primary force behind parking lot protocol is first noting there is such a thing, and secondly, not turning off your brain just because you are off the main road!

LUNDBERGism

There is nothing that is common or sensible to the person who does not grasp your version of what you think should be apparent in terms of the concept of "common sense".

Chapter 37
Seven Things to Know and Learn From You

"Whatever words we utter should be chosen with care for people will hear them and be influenced by them for good or ill." ~ Buddha

It is not from things that we learn, rather experiences, and most good experiences involve other people to some degree. Being a leader of at least one (yourself), and likely others formally by title, or informally by your presence and expertise, it is important to coach for learning. Regardless of how long people have been working with you, especially if they "report" to you, there are seven key things they are best to know and learn from you:

1. The reason he/she was hired. This is above and beyond the qualifications he/she displays, as it goes into the values you share, in your eyes making them perfectly suited to a great working partnership with you and your team. Elevate both their self-esteem and their sense of belonging by conveying the fit factors with each team member. Shared perspective is one of the things that you seek for common ground, and a business-partner mentality can be your approach to getting your team up to speed quickly and with ownership like no other group. When employees clearly understand the tasks they were hired to do, all future job objectives become much more meaningful. There is an expression I use often that reminds us that

people engage in a world most quickly and passionately when they were part of creating that world (people support a world they help create). So, let them know what drew you to them, and let them possibly share that back as well.

2. Your expectations for customer service inside your group/organization and outside it. How do you define customer service? What are some terrific examples within the company of such service? What are some examples of other companies' stellar service? What are the limits on satisfying the customer...financially and otherwise? Resist telling the story of the restaurant that serves only Pepsi products but allows servers to go to the store down the street to get a Coke product if the customer is set on Coke if you are basing your interactions/service solely on speed. Do tell that story if service is defined as wowing the customer. (I experienced this at a restaurant/brewery in the Mid-west.)

3. The best way to work with and for you. Employees are not telepathic...and neither are you! Share with them candidly how you work well and what does not fit for you. This will save days, weeks or months of annoying one another, or worse yet, an exit from the company from someone who felt it was not the right place to be when it was a simple lack of communication. Most of us are a little quirky and the majority of us know it, whether we like to admit it or not, and the strength in admitting it in these cases is that we can/will avoid issues that will, inevitably surface later.

4. The best approach to talking with you. Like seeks like, and when people do not know how to approach someone, language to use or avoid, etc., it is certain they will not get it right the first time. So, if you are a processor, and it takes a while to respond, let the others know so that if they are blurters and you are quiet, it does not mean they should just keep talking and hinder the communication. Also, if you are a person who discusses things more casually than scheduled meetings, while I do not recommend that fully, if that is your style for talking, it is best others know it.

5. That you want to know when/how they like to be recognized. This one is simple: ask and listen, and remember the response. It is likely that nobody, or very few people with whom you work, have been asked if they like to be recognized immediately, at special meetings, at the monthly call/meeting, on the phone, in person, etc. And, even less likely is how they like appreciation: verbally, in writing, through gift cards, plaques, etc. Give the parameters of what you have available through your company and let the other person choose.

<Slobification Snippet>
I was often the only female on a team in the auto industry, and the rewards for monthly/quarterly goal attainment were ties, golf shirts, etc. Those went to friends/family and were useless to me. Not until 15 years into my career did someone ask me...and I said gift cards to restaurants or home improvement stores...I'll pass on the ties, thanks.

And, boy was it a thrill when I received the gift cards for my accomplishments...they reinforced my work/effort, and that my leader listened.

6. How you view the company goals/vision. Sure, the mission statement is likely posted, but what, specifically, does it mean to you and/or your team. Share how you personally own it, and consistently demonstrate the behavior and choices you anticipate will get the group to that mission/vision.

7. That you care. Even if you botch the other six, which you will not, make sure the others on your team know you care. Care comes from asking how they are and really listening, not requesting "favors" and being available...including covering for them when they have a conflict, and asking about the spouse and kids by name...and yes, even looking at the vacation photos. These care times must be sincere so that a bond forms. Cared for people are likely to speak out, speak up, look out for others, stay, and care back.

So, while you think you are too busy for "leadership gimmicks", you are! Please know these are not gimmicks, rather valuable steps to forging relationships that create loyalty, interest, and learning. And, after all, people do not like to be taught, but they love to learn, so give someone a chance to learn today.

Chapter 38
Airport Antics

"A man wrapped up in himself
makes a very small bundle."
~Benjamin Franklin

Whether you travel a lot or a little, here is something to consider: the way people move through airports is a direct reflection of how they drive.

<Slobification Snippet>
While on a year of travel every six-to-eight weeks, I began to notice a few common occurrences in airports, including:

- *People walking in the middle or on the left side (we are in America, let's walk to the right to keep traffic flowing and avoid unnecessary contact/collisions).*
- *People dress as though they are already at a tiki hut.*
- *Conversations on phones are louder than ever, and far more boldly conveyed than deemed necessary (already discussed in earlier chapters).*
- *People cutting others off in a somewhat competitive nature with their bags in tow.*
- *Carrying more than allowed seems to be a personal challenge to some.*
- *The concept "I never!" comes out a lot when flights change.*
- *Rage seems to mount quickly, often, and without much warning. It seems as though*

the customer service and ticket counter
airline team members get the brunt of it!

I consistently watched some people stay in their lane while others cut people off while still more walk (drive) aimlessly at various speeds without any GPS...be alert at the airport...there are no yield signs, traffic lights, or blinkers near any frequent flier programs...and yet, oddly, there seems to be a bit of road rage...

These above mentioned antics were, and are, not the case with all travelers. Still, if you think about being in an airport, it is not a protective bubble where your communication, behaviors and relationships are on a "hall pass". The same is true for your vehicles. People at the airport are people first, not just passengers or other travelers. People in their cars, SUVs and trucks also are people, not just other defensive drivers. Let's keep that in mind in the concourses, and additionally when we get in our cars to drive wherever we are going!

Chapter 39
Gum - Sticky Topic

"Appearances are often deceiving."
~ Aesop

Have you ever been speaking to someone chewing gum and realize you are not listening, rather watching that pink, white, or blue wad of gum in his/her mouth float around? It's not only distracting to see something bounce around someone's teeth and tongue, it is practically hypnotic…if you have not been grossed out by it!

<Slobification Snippet>
While watching a coach of a team give an interview at a press conference that was not before or after a game, he drew me in with that oh-so-familiar stick of gum being chewed.

I was not drawn to listen, rather to question if he knew he was on TV as he sat in front of many reporters, if he cared that he showed no real interest in being professional, and if his breath was so bad that he would sacrifice a good conference to have people thinking about his gum and not his responses.

It really is a funny thing about gum...sure, it freshens breath, relieves dry mouths during workouts & provides fun for blowing bubbles in the privacy of homes or cars, but I've yet to find a person or documented statement that proclaimed gum made someone seem more attractive on a date, more intelligent in a meeting, more of a match in

...an interview, or more convincing in discussions, so perhaps reconsider it on certain occasions.

LUNDBERGism

Things don't just happen in life...people make them happen!

Chapter 40
Networking: A Full-Time, Full-Contact "Sport"

"We are caught in an inescapable network of mutuality, tied in a single garment of destiny. Whatever affects one directly, affects all indirectly." ~ Martin Luther King, Jr.

While there are a lot of suggestions for networking and attending various functions, there are few that I believe serve you best. You will find each of my suggestions are easy to remember, require action on your part and focus more upon the other person than upon yourself.

Just know, networking is not synonymous with communicating. It is your responsibility to make the other person feel connected and interested! Network by focusing your attention on results, and not just the action of being at an event. Before you use any of the ideas for networking, commit to the following:

1. If you go to a networking event with someone, agree to drive to and from the location together and have minimal (or even no) contact at the event. Having a conversation with your friend while at a networking event just means you wasted time and energy driving to the function when you could have just met where you usually do. If you want time with your buddy, go get a coffee or drink after the networking

function; just do not spend your time together since that is not productive!

2. Have enough cards for two per person you can potentially meet. Make sure those cards are up-to-date with no changes in name, email or phone scratched out and written in pen. Is the focus of your plan your career? If so, then get professional cards printed with minimally your name, email and phone with your 2-4 areas of professional expertise listed. Make sure your cards are only UV coated on the front so that people can make notes on the back.

3. Have easy access to your cards and place those you receive from others in an equally convenient location. Ladies…no purses at networking events, or at least carry small ones and ensure you do not need to fumble with zippers, etc. when getting your cards. Go for functionality at the events and use your pockets for your card and cardholders.

4. Check your attitude and outside interests at the door. Keep in mind the situation, opportunity and focus, and know that your truly do not get a second chance to make a first impression!

A quick way to remember how to communicate is with the acrostic for NETWORK:

Name. Locate the person in charge of the event a few days prior to the date. Ask for a list of attendees. Sometimes these lists will not be disclosed, but it's worth a shot. If you do not get the names, arrive early and review the nametags to come up with a plan for who you would like to meet. For your name, wear a name tag. Go ahead and have one made so that you are comfortable with it.

Event. No matter how long the networking event lasts, commit to attending minimally for an hour. When people "blow in" and "blow out", others notice. Additionally, staying at least one hour gives you the opportunity to catch latecomers. You already arrived early to see the names and prepare for whom you wish to meet. Now you are poised as the person whom others wish to meet.

Target. Target people or companies when you arrive early and plan for whom you want to interact. Target three-four solid connections for each hour you are at the engagement. This does not mean you can only speak with three-four people, but focus on quality over quantity. Collecting business cards is one thing…getting the perhaps few cards of people who can help further your bailout plan is another. This is communicating versus networking.

Work. Work the room. Yes, work it! This is where you take on the role of a host or co-host. This is not to say you take credit for the event or the party, rather you make it a point to welcome others and introduce them with a firm, quick handshake of two-to-four pumps of the hand, and interested, interactive conversation. When you appear as the person to meet, you become the person to meet.

Offer. Even though you are looking to advance in your area(s) of life focus and move forward with your plan at each networking event you attend, make sure you devote equal time and attention to listening to and learning about the other people you meet. They may also have areas of life focus and plans, and good communication is a two-way street. If your expertise can help someone else, they will be much more likely to help you. Make an offer to follow through with information, a contact or something else, and you will endear yourself to that person. When you follow up with him or her in the future, you are now a welcomed call, e-mail or letter coming across his or her desk, rather than another person just looking for a favor. This is a value position that must be sincere in the offer and quick in the execution.

Reach. You have made the new contact and figured out a value-added connection you can provide. Now be sure to reach back out to him or her after the event. Typically, a follow through outreach within 24 hours is optimal. Keep in mind, a phone call can appear pushy, and an e-mail can be impersonal. Contrarily, a handwritten note is quite personal, and a note with a relevant article or bit of information is a real connection (if you have agreed to follow up via phone or email do that, but if there is no commitment, go for the personal note). Think about it…how many people display, or even save, phone messages or emails? Not many. However, many of us keep handwritten notes as keepsakes because they create a personal connection.

Keep. It has been stated that you must network regularly…not just when you need something. Networking is a function that you must constantly keep on your weekly to-do lists, not just something to do if you need a new job or referral. Keep also stands for keeping in touch and keeping your word.

When a person says he or she will be somewhere or do something on a particular date and then lets it slide, this becomes memorable for all the wrong reasons. Keeping up with your commitments keeps progress on your plan going in the right direction!

With this tip and these tools, you will be networking sincerely, and with impact and results!

> ### LUNDBERGism
> Life *is* a contact sport.

Chapter 41
Réspondez S'il Vous Plaît

"The only man who is really free is the one who can turn down an invitation to dinner without giving any excuse."
~ *Jules Renard*

Are considerations and manners regarding RSVPs a thing of the past?

Not necessarily. With email, evite and text messaging, some people perceive a catered party the same as a social gathering at a home and likely the same as a happy hour at a bar/club...and there are clear differences! You will likely be invited back again and again if you follow the courtesies of the RSVP. Sadly, more and more often, (and through personal experience) hosts commonly do not receive solid indications whether guests plan to attend their events, even if RSVP is clearly denoted on the invitation or in the evite. Considering each person in a work or social group comes from a different background, family situation and exposure, perhaps revisiting what RSVP means is best first. The term RSVP (or more formally, R.S.V.P.) comes from the French expression "Réspondez S'il Vous Plaît", meaning "please respond" (or as I like to think of it, respond and then follow through if you ever want to maintain social graces).

If/when you get an invitation or evite with an RSVP indicator, it means you want to tell the host whether or not you plan to attend the party, and by the date indicated in the invitation. If there is no date indicated for a response, provide your firm reply as soon as possible, and minimally five (5) days prior to the event. RSVP does not mean to respond only if you're coming, and it does not mean respond only if you're not coming (the expression "regrets only" is reserved for that instance). An incomplete list of respondents can cause numerous problems for a host including difficulty in planning food quantities, issues relating to minimum guarantees with catering halls, uncertainty over the number of party favors and difficulties in planning appropriate seating, among other things. Also, do not invite other guests to attend a party if there is hosting of drinks or food involved. If you would like someone included, ask the host before five days prior if all the invitations have been sent. If your invitation indicates a guest, bring no more than one guest, and let the host know his/her name prior to arriving at the event. (The exception to this guideline is if there is a pay-as-you-go happy hour event that is not at someone's home, and/or if the host has indicated "the more the merrier" on the invitation.)

What happens if something unexpected comes up in the five days prior to the event or even the day of the event? Make an effort to phone the host as soon as you know you cannot attend (getting a more exotic offer is not a reason not to attend…ethics and decency should play into accepting an invitation). When you reach the host, do not bog him or her down with your story. Simply be brief, ask forgiveness and offer to pay for your portion of the festivities. Yes, you have committed and now you are backing out, so plan to provide relief to the host. Often the host will not accept payment. Send a note within the week and a small gift if the event was being catered. Flowers are a welcomed surprise and thoughtful way to keep things pleasant between you. A gift is not necessary…just a great touch! Remember, the host is investing in everything from glasses to favors and food. You being considerate of the fact that the seating and event/game counts may be off, is the least you can do!

When you do attend an event for which you have RSVP'd, take a small token of your appreciation, like a bottle of wine, spirits, or candle. Host gifts are wonderful and many a host loves to show them off in their home for it shows kindness and enjoyment and reminds them that people recognize them for opening their home. A host gift is not necessary, though. A call or note the next day will work as a close second for giving thanks to the host. Regardless of what you do, give thanks…and do not ask for a house tour if you are at the host home. Remember he/she has been working on the event…let him/her offer if they like. For all we know as the guest, one room became the "catch all" if you will, and the last thing the composed host should be put in a position to do is to have to explain the closed door to a room!

If you are hosting a party where you are providing food or drink…or both, I suggest including an RSVP to be written on an invitation or in an evite and do not text, or simply email an invitation. When the RSVP is noted, state a firm date for the responses. If you find many people hedge for a better offer, an opportunity, a child's possible event taking priority, then, when making your reminder calls (preferred over emails, but emails are

Okay…minimally do some sort of reminder or confirmation), just let people know at that three-to-five days prior period that while you would love to have them there, you'll put them as a no for this event and perhaps the next time scheduling will work out better. Do not accept a maybe only a few days out. While you may have enough food and drink, it sets the stage for repeated behavior by that person…and sets the example for far too many more!

What happens if something unexpected comes up in the five days prior to the event or even the day of the event and someone has not canceled and you are the host expecting him or her? Make an effort to phone or email the MIA guest as soon as the next day. Please do not assume the person blew off your party/event, rather something may have happened that was tragic, so let's keep things in perspective with verbiage like that which is shared on the next page.

Subject: Checking in After Your RSVP

Hi There (Name)!

Good morning! Hopefully you are doing well. We had a ball yesterday celebrating, and, as a courtesy, I included you in the photo sharing (if you took pictures and use a photo sharing site, of course). You were missed at the party for which your RSVP was yes, and we were concerned when we did not see you, get a text, a phone call, an email, or even a change on the evite to inform us of your not planning to attend.

If something happened and you want/need assistance, please let me know...certainly I will make myself available and gladly lend a hand. Otherwise, after not hearing anything in advance of the party (or even during the bash) and making arrangements for you to be included in all the festivities, please know that we will not likely extend future invitations to our place for our hosted/catered events. We certainly still look forward to seeing you out and catching up at other parties/places.

See you soon...make it a great start to a reflective and productive week...

Regards,

Your Name
Phone Number
Email address

Providing this offers accountability that the guest clearly lacked. On the other hand, should something terrible have arisen, you are showing genuine concern and an offer to assist. Either way, the peace is kept and the boundaries are set so that there are no hard feelings, no mixed messages are communicated, and a neglected RSVP is less likely to happen in the future.

So, having taken all this in, remember, the next time you see RSVP on an invitation you receive, do just that, Réspondez S'il Vous Plait, promptly and make it a spectacular party/event!

Chapter 42
Charity for Giving...and Getting!

"Where there is charity and wisdom, there is neither fear nor ignorance."
~ St. Francis of Assisi

It's almost as though the idea of giving back is supposed to be unique and almost auspicious, and yet there are so many simple, yet thoughtful and thorough ways to invest in your community, and really, in the long run, invest in you…from a heart and soul perspective.

By giving back, I don't mean writing a check (which is terrific, too, so I am not negating the impact, just focusing elsewhere on this blog entry!).

Not sure where/how to give? If you haven't lately, consider:

1. Taking inventory of the things for which you are grateful.

2. Recording all the people's names who positively influenced you and how.

3. Noting all things you are good at doing.

From those three lists, you will have a clear picture of what means the most to you, how you got there, and an action/sharing you can contribute. Perhaps you are grateful for being healthy, your grandfather was a painter who encouraged you with words and insights, and you are good with a roller…that is a super combination for "Paint Your Heart Out" or another painting style charity. The same would be true for you if you have a love of music, you had a music teacher who inspired you and you are very effective with children…perhaps you could volunteer for a church or after-school program about music education.

Whatever your triad of lists reveals, take action on it…and watch the difference you make in your community, with those you impact, and even in yourself. After all, there's an old adage that reminds us that charity begins at home…let your home base be charitable in a way that works for many!

LUNDBERGism

Give freely, give generously, give from your heart and your head, and then give some more. If you are ever in doubt…give…it will all come back to you somehow, some way, and likely in a way you could never imagine, and with so much added joy to all who were involved!

Section 3:
Thriving
Relationships

"Don't smother each other.
No one can grow in the
shade." ~ Leo Buscaglia

It is likely your first relationship was that with one or both of your parents, or a relative of sorts. These relationships can be nurturing or taxing...or both. Thriving relationships are not only possible, they are probable when intent, attitude, actions, awareness, forgiveness, humility, a sense of humor combine (that's all?). For thriving relationships, one must want them, work for them, and be appreciative of them. Unlike the parental relationship, most rapport is not born, it is grown and cultivated. It is both communication, and behaviors that impact relationships, and in this section, a bit of a different twist is taken on the types of words and ways tips you have read earlier.

Chapter 43
Memorability...It's Up to You

"Pleasure is the flower that passes;
remembrance, the lasting perfume."
~ Jean de Boufflers

How is it some things, some people, some events,
are more memorable than others? Are they more
graphic, more loud, more extravagant? Perhaps one
or all of those things rings true, still, the concept of
memorability is one I suggest you take on for
you...about you.

Consider this, when people do not remember your
name, it is not entirely because they are "bad with
names" (which is an overly used, and even more
sadly, an overly accepted excuse for not recalling
names), rather it is likely a combination of their
self-interest or disinterest and your lack of
memorability. Yes, it is true, in order to be
memorable, you may want to work at being
memorable!

What do I mean by memorable? Extremely good
and extremely bad things are remembered most.
Think about it for 30-60 seconds, you will almost
assuredly recall something tremendously wonderful
or something that nears disgust when given the
opportunity for something to enter your mind.
Having recognized that, your charge is to keep your

impression on others in the former, rather than the latter, category!

Begin with your approach…smile at the other person, the most common reply to a smile is one in kind. Then, as you go to state your name, say it like the other person has never said it (remember, they have not!)…meaning directly and informatively. Use the Red/Yellow/Green approach by thinking stop (Red), proceed slowly (Yellow), giving time and breath after your first name, and then go (Green) ahead with your last name. Make the time and effort to connect with names. When it is not your turn, rather than think internally "wow, I did that just right", just listen, as the person with whom you are interacting is saying his or her name. If you are busy in self-praise, you are likely to miss the other person's name. While I mentioned your memorability being in your hands, giving your name clearly is only one part…remembering the other person's is another. Often people will reply that they like someone they do not know well simply after that person has called him or her by name. Yes, repeating the other person's name three times assists in your recall. Yes, writing down the person's name is helpful. And, yes, the most important part of remembering a name is actually hearing it in the first place!

So, while you are using the person's name appropriately, and you are getting to know him or her, resist asking about what the person does as the second inquiry (the first being his/her name). People are so much more than what they do, yet the second most commonly asked question I hear from others (after "what is your name?"), is "what do you do?". Asking a question like that begins to center your conversation around work, and people's occupations are not always the most likeable, and therefore, not the most memorable part about them. Stick with open-ended questions that spark enthusiasm and/or excitement, such as "(Name), what is it that keeps your attention when you are not at work?", or "What do you like to do in your free time?". It is almost certain that someone will reply "I am always at work" or "Free time, what is that?", yet the majority of people will go to their areas of enjoyment/passion quickly and engage in some enriching conversation with you...making you most memorable to them!

Finally, at an appropriate point in the conversation, should you want to network, maintain a connection, or even build on making a friend, a typical form of sharing information is the business card exchange. Keep your business cards handy. Digging in your suit or bag or wallet to pull out a half-mangled version of a once lovely card may make you memorable...and not in the way this tip is intending.

When you have your card in your hand, put your thumb under it with your fingers on top of it (much like a top and bottom frame) and present it to the other person with the card outstretched toward the other person near the height level of your face. In other words, banish the thumb on the top of your card, waist level pass to their hand. The point of the "framing of the card" near your face is to lock in the lasting impression of you and your name with the person receiving it.

It is likely you will get the other person's card in the flawed way of meekly providing a card in a fashion similar to a Las Vegas dealer distributing playing cards, that is fine…just adjust quickly by holding it out, reading it, and commenting on it so that the other person knows you took the time to remember him or her. (Think back to how many times you or someone else did not read a business card…it is awkward and a bit of a let down to an otherwise often good experience.) Place the card in a holder, or in the same place from which you retrieved your card to show the importance of the card to you.

Throughout this memorability coaching, please know that none of this will work without sincerity and interest. In other words, being memorable is not a popularity contest, rather a show of genuine intent and follow through. So, the next time someone doesn't remember your name (which if I were a betting person, I'd say will be happening less and less once you create a habit of this tip), instead of thinking they were not interested, reflect on how interesting you were…and improve on that, making you most memorable for the next time!

LUNDBERGism

There is a certain point in the day where you decide "Yes, this is the way I want to present myself to the world today." Own it!

Chapter 44
Five P's to Marketing You

"It is very important to generate a good attitude, a good heart, as much as possible. From this, happiness in both the short term and the long term for both yourself and others will come." ~ Dalai Lama

When marketing a product, the five Ps are:

Product
Price
Place (Distribution)
Promotion
People

And, I believe *You* are your product, so the five Ps in marketing you are:

Positive
Passionate
Present
Professional
Personable

Strive to be *positively passionate* as a *present professional* who is *personable* in all you do, and sales, and repeat sales will be generated with much more enjoyable efforts, and with less "work".

Remember, you are selling *you* first, and then the products/services you have to offer and represent will likely be more interesting and relevant as well!

LUNDBERGism

Sell yourself from the inside out...after all, Product One *is* You!

Chapter 45
Take Advantage of Anger for "Good"

"If you are patient in one moment of anger, you will escape a hundred days of sorrow." ~ Chinese Proverb

You get angry, I get angry, anger is a part of life. I would love to share with you ways to never be angry, and yet that is not realistic.

What is realistic is having an approach and being prepared for what may be, and avoiding what we would ultimately not want to have happened.

Consider anger is real, it comes from somewhere, and ultimately anger can either guide us to succeed or fail in how we recognize it, process it, and manage it. Think ANGER in these terms for fully working through how you want to handle it:

Allow yourself to be angry. Watch beating yourself up and/or expecting yourself to be positive, perfect (no such thing, really, since each individual and situation begets new perspectives and ideas, as we are in perpetual change).

Name the anger. From where does it come and what is it? Get in touch with it so you know whether of not you are reacting or responding, and if you are directed by what is in front of you or other issues lurking.

Give yourself an amount of time to be angry and then come back to it.

Exit the scene, conversation, or scenario to save face, preserve grace, and decide your pace.

Resolve your issue with whatever or whomever angered you by addressing it with a solution, an agreement to disagree, or severing of the relationship/experience (may sound harsh, and yet you know, intuitively what is likely best once you have space/time and perspective.)

By being prepared for navigating anger, it will not negate it or avoid it, rather it will give you a realistic approach for when that discomfort arises.

LUNDBERGism

If we speak when we are angry, we are likely in for more talking later...beginning with an apology. Take a breath, walk away, and then come back to calm-speak and conversation instead of anger-speak and disrespect.

Chapter 46
10 Ways to Compel through Connection!

"There are no traffic jams along the extra mile." ~ Roger Staubauch

While there is much talk about how to serve clients, below are 10 ways to truly make a connection. This approach means not just customer service, it means client care. This means not just reacting to a situation, it means responding to the person in the situation. Often we think we want to tell people about something, but that is just chatter, and then we make the attempt to sell them on an idea, but that has a lot to do with convincing and persuasion, and if we reach a level where someone is compelled to work with us and/or partner with us as a client or customer, then we have built a relationship through true rapport!

1. Wow them with your words, and make them ambassadors through your actions. Say what you mean and do what you say you will do. Offer incentives and ask for referrals. Welcome people back instead of asking where have YOU been? No need to discount you or your product, instead, show appreciation with special offers/opportunities.

2. Think and say "Yes, and", and demonstrate an "Absolutely I can" attitude. Start positive and stay positive. Focus on what is RIGHT versus what is WRONG. Be humble in your errors and show moxie in your solutioning. Have fun in what you do.

3. Plant the SEED (Strive to Exceed Expectations Denoted) for Success. You have to know what is expected to meet/exceed the expectation. Be humane...not just human.

4. Know your "difference", live your truth and be memorable. Remember the win is not just in getting a customer, it is also about keeping customers. Each client's perception of you and/or your company will determine how well you do this and that perception will depend on how compelling you are to them. Make things a memorable experience. The connection of knowing someone's name and smiling sincerely are great for a start. Leave people with something they either cannot get elsewhere or cannot get in a way you deliver it. Know your two-four areas of expertise and stick with them. Otherwise, say "no thank you", and connect, connect, connect as the referral source.

5. Get and Give Feedback. Take notes, use names, and really listen. Listen to understand instead of just to react. If you are a challenged listener, notes will slow your pace. Agree with a person and disagree with an idea (not the other way around). When you survey your clients, and I encourage surveying, share the results quickly and without defense. Own the results and state the actions you'll take...and then do just that!! Address the issue at hand, and then dig into the root cause.

6. Adopt a no-corner-cutting mentality/approach. If you already have one, let everyone know! Our society is about "gimme more"...and what

else can I get. Be the one with the integrity to walk away.

7. Give back...for the right reasons. Checks are nice, actions make a difference, and advocacy allows for learning. People like to do business with people who are more than just business. Earn their respect and then share about charities/groups for the reason of advocacy and learning...not just to get recognized or to be a top fund-raiser. Strive for fun-raising instead, and your give-backs will get more!

8. Appropriately promise and appropriately deliver (Instead of under-promise and over-deliver, also know as "sandbagging"). Be a business of both empowerment and accountability. Offer options...only two-three and only those with which you are okay.

9. Strive for inclusivity instead of exclusivity. There is a difference in when people are part of something versus people attempting to "get in" where there is a level of discomfort. Make people feel welcomed and a part of your success.

10. Know that the quality of customer service cannot exceed the quality of the people who provide it. Your team, even if you are a team of one, will treat others how they are treated. Start with a positive view of you...that view carries far! There is a connection with how we feel about ourselves and how we care for others. Invest in you/your team a set % of earnings, and only let that grow as your success grows!

Pick and choose what works for you in your situation. How can you enhance your customer and client relationships through care and connection? After all, aren't we all about compelling customers and clients to drive client satisfaction and genuinely connect with us?

LUNDBERGism

Believe in yourself first…it makes it more compelling for others to follow suit!

Chapter 47
Respect – Not from Age, Rather From Actions

"He who wants a rose must respect the thorn." ~ Persian Proverb

While I write a lot about "Reversing the Slobification of America"™, I do not mean it only is an issue for youth, generation X or Y or any one group, for that matter!

Respect or lack of respect are often a reflection of how you feel about yourself, and while I am happy and respectful, I do not believe that children or adults can demand respect for their age or position, rather it should follow from their actions and personal leadership.

<Slobification Snippet>
I was at an independent living facility and was moving things (in for my Grandparents) when a woman came up and basically refused to walk around the items being moved or act friendly in any way. I was chipper and greeted her with a "Good Morning", and then she and her cat, in a baby stroller, waited in the blazing sun for me to move about 40 pounds of things so that she did not have to go around in the clean grass or down the small curb. I did not mind, but thought how sad she chose to be...poor cat, too...

The same day, less than an hour later, another woman came upon us moving with different things in the way. Again, I was chipper and greeted her with a "Good Morning", and much to my joy and pleasure, she responded in kind. When I quickly tended to moving things, she said not to worry and that she was just fine walking below. Her openness and attitude reminded me, once again, that it is all in the way we approach things.

Who do I respect? Seemingly needless to say, the second woman. I am stating it, though, just to give her double the credit for acting in a respectful way!

Believe me, I was raised to respect my elders, and approach them that way at first and look for it to continue. Respect, after all, is a two-way street...even if it is a bit crowded with a new neighbor's moving items...

LUNDBERGism

Compliment *consistently*,
and only criticize *constructively*.

Chapter 48
...By Any Other Name...

"Let us make distinctions, call things by the right names." ~ Henry David Thoreau

It's been heard repeatedly that a rose by any other name is still a rose, right? While that may be true for a flower and even people, our knowing what we are, is important, and others recognizing who we are, makes a difference, too. In the chapter on being memorable, it was conveyed that how your name matters in whether or not someone remembers your name and/or remembers you. Similarly, whether a group of people work *with* you or *for* you, remember to call each of them by name, as people appreciate a personal touch. Nicknames like "honey" or "buddy" should be avoided. Gender specific nicknames, if you are intrigued by using them, should be substituted for the other gender in your mind...either you'll laugh or roll your eyes...and either way, you'll see the silliness and lack of consideration it conveys when you use them.

Should you find yourself in a position where someone's name escapes you, simply say "because your name is so important, please share it with me again". This message, and admission of neglecting to recall the person's name, is not only honest, it shows humility and genuine care and interest. The same is true for the pronunciation of a name. You are encouraged to state "because your name is so important, please share the pronunciation with me again." People are less likely to be annoyed, and most likely pleased that you took the time to show interest and ask, rather than just mumble a name, not call them by name, or avoid them all together, like so many others have done.

Finally, when referring to a group/team in conversation with others, say "our team" or even "my group" versus "my people" or "my staff" in order to show respect and collaboration instead of superiority/position.

These things allow people to sense your confidence, and recognize your professionalism...and possibly even follow your lead!

Chapter 49
Eliminating "I Don't Have Time"

"You will never 'find' time for anything. If you want time, you must make it." ~ Charles Bruxton

Strike the words "I don't have time" from your vocabulary. Yes, you read that correctly. Nobody won a time lottery and got 25 hours and likewise, no one lost the time lottery and was awakened one day with only 22 hours. So, call it like it is and let people know the truth.

When the expression "I don't have time", and even "I am too busy", comes into play, it is really conveying that the person stating that has no control over his or her time…and that person is, in effect, out of control.

What to do?

Replace the "I don't have time" excuse with "that is not a priority for me right now, I will get to it tomorrow (the next day, etc.) or "while I would like to assist, my calendar is full and I have availability on Tuesday" or if it comes from your manager/leader, simply ask, "Please assist me in prioritizing these things, as I have a full day planned, but will gladly adjust to moving something to tomorrow or the day after". This is not rude…this is truthful.

Keep in mind, if you want to get something done, you find a way and if you don't, you find an excuse.

Excuses are crutches. You are a healthy individual with 24 hours each day, so make no excuses, make your time count consistently…you just did by investing time in this book, and not being too busy to implement the tips.

In the long run, your colleagues, friends, and family will respect and appreciate your approach, and surprisingly, you will be in control and you, too, will respect and appreciate your approach!

Chapter 50
Four Questions Many Leaders Overlook

"People who ask confidently get more than those who are hesitant and uncertain. When you've figured out what you want to ask for, do it with certainty, boldness and confidence." ~ Jack Canfield

Want to connect with each of your team members at work, in your family, and in volunteer positions? You likely do so many things to do just that, and in addition, you have already read many ways to make that effort in this book.

For one more, ensure you know (by know, I mean ask each person directly) these following four questions that I find many leaders overlook:

1. What's going well for you here (at company, in relationship, as a volunteer)?

2. What would you like to see improved here (at company, in relationship, as a volunteer)?

3. What keeps you working here?

4. What would make you leave here (the company, relationship, volunteer role)?

Listen to the responses.
By learning these four things, you'll know what matters to those impacting your customers/clients &

your bottom line, family dynamics, your services and charitable endeavors, and then, you can take appropriate action based on the feedback!

LUNDBERGism

If you are making progress, you're making some errors, but that's okay, you're also making strides, and no doubt, you are making a difference!

Chapter 51
What a Difference a Mood Makes!

"Nothing helps a bad mood like spreading it around." ~ Bill Watterson

Being around people often once a week, some individuals I see more often than that, and it is interesting how an "outsider" can see "in"!

One thing that is clear is that a mood makes a difference. You are responsible for your mood, and stating "I am in a bad mood" is not good enough. Decide your mood and embrace it.

<Slobification Snippet>
Have you ever 'experienced' the person who I will call an "Energy Vampire"? He or she is the person who acts as though a favor is being done by greeting you (and especially if it is part of his or her role/job). That same person hates the weather if it too hot and despises the cold, sees the rain only for the wet roads and not the nutrition to the soil, and basically sucks the energy out of a room.

You do not need to be "in a great mood", but if you want to be in an open mood or reflective mood, then do that instead. The idea of a good mood and a bad mood makes it look and feel like there are only two.

Let your mood be yours and know that you own it, it impacts others to some degree, and that looking back, your mood is not an excuse for how you behaved, rather a reference to what you chose to be/have that day!

Chapter 52
Loving You, and All You Do!

"An occasional compliment is
necessary to keep up one's self-
respect." ~ Mark Twain

How many times have you gotten home from school
or work and thought "well, I am just so full of
compliments and recognition today, I think I am
full!"? What? Not often? Never? Well, while it is
a shame that we do not receive accolades often and
in a timely manner from others, it is not everyone
else's fault that we do not feel appreciated.

Want to get over that sense of needing recognition
from others? After you are done doing what you
are doing, (reading this book, right?) please do the
following:

1. Make a list of the most influential people to you.

2. Make a list of your top three strengths.

3. Write a note that reads something like this:

Hi (Name)!

Thank you for being an important part of my life!

In order to grow personally, I am soliciting your feedback
regarding me. Please let me know what you see as my top
three strengths.

I look forward to your reply on or before xx/xx/xx (date one
week from the date of the letter). Meanwhile, make it a great
day!

Regards,
Your Name
Your Email
Your Phone Number

4. Email or mail the notes to those living, who are on your list (minimally three).

When you receive the notes and/or emails back, hand write or type the strengths sent to you and close the list with your top three. Please email or mail a note to those who responded with something similar to:

Hello (Name)!

Thank you for your response to my request for a listing of my top strengths.

I see your strengths as 1)_____ 2) _____ and 3 _____. I appreciate you recognized mine as _____, _____, and _____.

Based on your input and others of importance to me, the list that I will use to reinforce my strengths is: (list all). You have once again made a difference in my life, and for this, I am grateful.

With appreciation, make it a memorable day!

Regards,
Your Name
Your Email
Your Phone Number

Post this list somewhere that you will see it…on a mirror, in the shower, in a drawer you open daily, as your screen saver, etc., and read it each day. When you read it, resist defending or denying the comment/strength, rather state I AM in front of each item on the list every day.

By becoming our own biggest fan, we rely less on the exterior world for reinforcement and more on ourselves and those of importance/influence to us personally, to guide and impact us...which is a lot more loving than hoping, wishing and longing for it at school or work. Then, when you receive praise elsewhere, it is a bonus, and maybe you'll want to add what you hear to your list!

Continue to love you and all you do, and believe me, you will become or continue to be that person who does recognize, praise, and appreciate others...right along with yourself!

LUNDBERGism

Be selfish...when you take care of yourself, *nobody else has to*!

Chapter 53
The Ten Minute Rule

"Being in control of your life and having realistic expectations about your day-to-day challenges are the keys to stress management, which is perhaps the most important ingredient to living a happy, healthy and rewarding life." ~ Marilu Henner

The *Ten Minute Rule*…what is *that*?

If you want to avoid mobile phone calls and/or other distractions when traveling to meet someone, when making plans, use the *Ten Minute Rule*.

The *Ten Minute Rule* is a 10-minute window of time when you are going to be somewhere or meet and as long as you are going to make that window, there is no need to rush/call, etc.

For example, if you want to meet a friend at 1:00 PM, and you are not sure of traffic and other delays, you could agree to meet between 1:00 PM and 1:10 PM, or 10 minutes to 1:00 PM and 1:00 PM.

Using the *Ten Minute Rule* with friends and family (not as widely suggested for business meetings) gives you a little bit of time to adjust to delays, keeps you "on time" within that window, and just solves the issue of that frantic phone call or text from traffic.

Chapter 54
Availability...Your Own Time Parameters

"All time management begins with planning." ~ Tom Greening

Does it seem like "time is getting away" from you, or that there "isn't enough time in the day"?

Imagine if you set a plan for your days including sleep time, preparation time, driving/commuting time, time for goals, working out, meals and family. You will likely be surprised by how much time is in that same 24 hours we each get each day.

The formula is short and completing the fields takes only a bit of time. The idea is to start at the top with what you want in your day, and then see what is left for work

Because time is a non-renewable resource, decide how much time you want to spend with your family/friends BEFORE thinking about your work day. Decide how many nights or weekend days you are committing to only your family/friends, and set that as your norm. Yes, you may make exceptions for weekly travel, etc., but overall, when you have a parameter on your time, and communicate that to both the people who you chose as your family and your work colleagues, people learn to respect it. Heck, they might even follow your example!

Very important as well is the fact that when you are working, you will be dedicated and committed to that time and focus, as you have planned for it, and not be distracted by how or when you will "make time" for your friends, social life and/or family. Your productivity, and therefore, your results, will rise with your respect and appreciation for your time and scheduling.

Here is the format to follow for what I call your "Availability", as we each have 24 hours in the day.

	24
Sleep	____
Family (Friends)	____
Downtime ("Me" Time)	____
Prep, Travel & Meals	____
Workout/Meditation	____
Goals/Studies/Planning	____
Other _____	____

Work is what is left!   ____

Track this each day for a week and make adjustments from the results. Watch how after 21-28 days, you have a renewed, or heck, it might be a brand new, appreciation and respect for you time. Since we all have the same amount of time in a day...this reminds us that it is what we CHOOSE to do with that time that makes the difference in our outlook, balance, pacing and, ultimately, our happiness.

LUNDBERGism

Nobody wins a "time lottery" and gets more hours in the day, so the excuse "I'm busy" or "I was too busy" just means you think your time is more valuable than mine.

Chapter 55
Intent Versus Results

"The leadership instinct you are born with is the backbone. You develop the funny bone and the wishbone that go with it." ~ Elaine Agather

When interacting with people, we often hear them say "you know what I meant", or "that is not what I meant to say". These people would like us to focus on something that is not there, but that we should somehow know.

It is appreciated that how things are intended are not consistently the way they are demonstrated or perceived. But, the reality is that intent is tough to measure and results are what are most easily tracked and/or measured.

Three things that will assist you in your processing various happenings are:

1. Consider someone's intent before responding, or otherwise, you are just reacting;

2. Measure the implication and results within a reasonable state and situation,

And, likely, the most important part…

3. Check your intent when doing or saying something…if you are doing or saying something to "stir the pot" or prove you are right, the result only serves you.

When your intent is to educate, improve and/or grow as a result (questions/clarification/caution), then, regardless of the result, it is best you ask and/or act.

While results may be the measurable part of action, the intent has its place...so keep it in mind for your leadership of self and others!

LUNDBERGism

Life isn't about what happens TO you, it's about what you make of what happens FOR you!

Chapter 56
Curbing Conflict

"Peace is not the absence of conflict but the presence of creative alternatives for responding to conflict -- alternatives to passive or aggressive responses, alternatives to violence." ~ Dorothy Thompson

When there is a conflict in your midst, consider these things before RESPONDING:

1. Is this about me?

2. What is this about...really?

3. Is this within my control?

4. Am I calm now?

5. Is it best to request discussing this later?

After that 10-20 seconds of self questioning, proceed with:

1. BTS – Breath, Tilt, Smile…this is the act of inhaling (to calm yourself), tilting your head slightly (to make you demeanor and presence a bit more approachable), and smiling to the degree that the smile is real and welcoming. This action will keep you from reacting, buy you a bit of time, so to speak, and bridge your inner thoughts to outer actions.

2. A calm, opening with the other person's name (watch tone!!).

3. Resist stating "I agree", if you do not, or "I understand", since you likely do not.

4. Offer, "What I heard was", or "Is it fair to start over with this and come up with a solution amidst our disagreement?"

5. Keep the discussion about the topic, not the person.

6. Communicate and continue to strive for a resolution/solution.

7. If no resolution/solution is reached, resist throwing up your arms or commenting snidely, rather request a revisit or to have another person decide or get involved.

8. Once a resolution/solution is reached, sincerely thank the other person for how he/she handled the situation professionally (not just for his/her time).

9. Follow through with what you two (or more) decided and be supportive of the decision even if it was not what you wanted.

Keep sight on what your focus is. This will allow you to determine what it is worth to continue to strive to be right versus what it is worth to move forward and make it a worthwhile and healthy exchange.

Chapter 57
Dumping or Delegating?

"Delegating work works, provided the one delegating works, too."
~ Robert Half

It is imperative you look at delegating as it is defined here, by me, for the purposes of training, coaching and/or workshops, rather than a direct dictionary definition, and stay away from dumping.

Definition of delegation: An act of collaboration and trust which involves assigning a result and opportunity along with the necessary responsibility and authority in order to successfully accomplish the desired result.

Embrace	Avoid
• Planning by establishing goals and performance standards for the result • Describing the result and expected outcomes, without the exact steps to follow • Identifying team members' strengths and areas of interest • Delegating authority along with responsibility • Assigning entire projects when possible, not just portions of things • Keeping communication open and respectful • Reinforcing success by providing recognition in a timely manner and approach	• Delegating H.R. issues (reviews, disciplinary action, colleague conflicts, etc.) • Being afraid of delegating too much—remember to match your leadership style to the individual's development level and allow growth and learning on both sides • Expecting perfection the first time...or at all times • Allowing team members a "feast" or "famine" period • Dictating how the result should be done • Delegating to the same person (people) all the time • Taking credit for others' actions/accomplishments

Keeping these guidelines in mind, and in practice, your leadership expands as it releases a hold on things/people...at the same time members of your team explore and soar in their own experience/success.

After all, as Dwight D. Eisenhower said, "You do not lead by hitting people over the head - that's assault, not leadership." Keep delegating, keep leading!

LUNDBERGism

Thinking leads to theories,
and actions yield results.

Chapter 58
Only Fools Rush Into Blame!

"Respect for character is always diminished in proportion to the number among whom the blame or praise is to be divided." ~ James Madison

Ever feel foolish? Embarrassed? Not in control? Who hasn't?

While each of us has likely experienced each of those things, we all handle them differently...

When we feel foolish, or made a fool of, it is imperative that we do not finger point and place blame...immediately or otherwise. While that may relieve the feeling of foolishness momentarily, it just shifts it in the eyes of those involved to insecurity or utter incompetence...and isn't that worse than the brief (and seemingly not-so-brief) foolishness?

As has been said many times in numerous situations, honesty is the best policy. When red-faced, caught without the answer, words, or your perceived sanity, remember, be honest. A great thing to do is BTS (Breath, Tilt, Smile), and say, "While that wasn't what I anticipated, let's see..." That shows composure, buys you some time, so to speak, and keeps you in control of you...even if the situation feels out of control!

Another thing to say with a sincere smile on your face is "this is awkward, and not insurmountable, so let's take a look at what is really happening here. I feel confident there is a solution or resolution." This allows others to know you are not attempting to cover things or side-step the issue, and also gives you latitude to assess and adjust.

Tap dancing, as it is often referred to, is not the best solution, although it is far improved over blame or denial. Ignoring something and shifting the focus is the precursor to the "800-pound gorilla in the room", and when the moment, presentation or conversation is done, tap dancing doesn't address the beast, rather it just moves it around a bit.

So, whether it is April Fools' Day, or any other day of the year, keep in mind what Albert Einstein proclaimed, "Anger dwells only in the bosom of fools."

With that, let's neither be angry nor blame, and simply own our outcomes. Accept responsibility, and be none the more foolish for any of it!

LUNDBERGism

Negativity breeds "why me?" thinking, where positivity leads to forward thinking, and an optimistic outlook of "what's next?".

Chapter 59
Forgive...And Not Forget...Rather, Learn?

"The existence of forgetting has never been proved: we only know that some things do not come to our mind when we want them to."
~ Friedrich Nietzsche

When something happens personally or professionally that does not seem fair, kind, or appropriate, there are varying levels of processing the experience. When something is silly or simply odd, that is typically categorized as annoying. When something elevates to irritation or inappropriate words or actions, it steps up the processing and responding to upsetting. At the point where things get personal or cost a company significant money without regard for feelings or outcomes, there is disappointment.

With all of these categories, it is a great idea to consider the person and his/her intent, results, and ownership of the situation. While I have previously written, and stand true to the fact that results are often far more important and lasting than intent, intent still is a consideration.

It is palatable to forgive, and possible even to forget, when all three...intent, results, and ownership, are embraced by the person in question. Less likely is the forgetting, and not necessarily recommended, when you are at a level of disappointment.

What to do? Consider the impact on you, others, and that person. Assess what you can do to improve/manage the situation, and do it. Request ownership if it has not been clear. Forgive the person for the situation, and I prefer to not forget, but rather learn from the situation.

One discussion on the topic is enough to put the experience in the past and use it as a guide and learning tool rather than a constant reminder of what "might" happen in the future. The worst things to do are to either not discuss it and just keep it inside, or tell the person what was wrong (versus interacting), or using the mistake as a tool for ridicule in the future.

Yes, the best predictor of future behavior is past behavior, but then again, the human race is the one where learning is possible, so forgive and learn, and see where that gets you, your perspective and your energy level for moving forward!

Chapter 60
Overcoming and Even Embracing FEAR

"He has not learned the lesson of life who does not every day surmount a fear." ~ Gaius Julius Ceasar

When we are afraid, we do not face fears/worries and address them, rather we allow them to own us and manifest into more concerns that paralyze or make us somewhat paranoid!

The real question is *what is FEAR?*

From what I can tell, FEAR is a four-letter word, so to speak, and some of the accurate descriptions of the past have included:

1. Failure Expected And Received

2. False Evidence Appearing Real

3. False Expectations About Reality

4. Finding Excuses And Reasons

Whatever you have allowed it to be, resist any of those above and embrace FEAR, the FEAR that is positively positioned to enhance your life, which is:

Facing
Each
Apparent
Resistance

You do this through first getting the information. This data gathering assists you in knowing what is real versus perceived. You stop speculating and anticipating while you are uncovering and learning. If you are unsure about something said or done, explore/ask until you are clear. From there, create and share a plan to move forward. Once shared, own only your part...in other words, resist over-committing.

Stay in touch with the steps and work the plan. With all this in mind, you can, and should, expect results without negative fear holding you back or sending you in a direction that is not warranted, rather by using positive and useful FEAR to your advantage!

LUNDBERGism

Some of the best fights "not lost" are those that you do not fight...let go of something someone said or did so you can be the biggest of winners!

Chapter 61
Confirm the WHOLE Picture

"Truth is confirmed by inspection and delay; falsehood by haste and uncertainty." ~ Publius Cornelius Tacitus

With the following questions in mind, and in use, when you request something of a team member, you will be far more likely than without them to get confirmation and agreement regarding the results you are seeking and the responsibilities and their owners.

1. Do you know **W**hat results are expected? (If not, share perspective and assignment/delegation again.)

2. Do you know **H**ow to do it? (If not, show how, and coach until clear or commit to providing tools.)

3. Do you agree you **O**wn this? (If not, walk through until there is ownership.)

4. Do you know the **L**ead-time for completion? (If not, share importance of the timing.)

5. Are we in agreement on these **E**xpecations? (Reiterate them, and this becomes a final follow through on all aspects.)

Use these questions after you have presented your proposal or request. These are reassurances for you

190

and the person with whom you are engaging in efforts. Asking these five questions will save you far more than five minutes later...and without offense or confusion as to what is desired...you will have the WHOLE picture!

LUNDBERGism

We are where we are based on choices
we have made.

Chapter 62
How to Get Idea Collaboration

"Resilience is really about collaboration and mutual understanding." ~ Roger Simpson

The world is not perfectly balanced, and that is both factual and unfortunate at times. Still, there are situations where balance may not be optimal, and yet collaboration and participation are essential for moving forward positively and collectively.

When faced with a differing opinion than yours or a group of people, remember to first review the objective of the plan/approach, and then secondly, ask of each group/party:

1. What about the idea/plan that will work for you? (or what is one thing about the idea/plan that will work for you?)

2. What about the idea/plan that is not a fit for you?

3. What solution do you propose now that you have heard all options?

While someone may answer nothing, everything, and mine, respectively, most people will be reasonable and there will be conversations and exchanges that lead to collaboration rather than a battle.

It is important to remember the objective, agree on that objective and then focus on the outcome, client, end-user, and results by means of approach. *After all, it is not about winning and losing, rather the solution that is best.*

LUNDBERGism

Instead of thinking of "working with someone" as a series of compromises and recalling only what you gave up, view your combined efforts as collaboration, and stay focused on what you both got out of it - the results!

Chapter 63
Differences Need Not Be Disastrous

"Honest differences are often a
healthy sign of progress."
~Mahatma Gandhi

It happens…we have misunderstandings,
differences arise, or communication creates
discomfort. Surely these interactions are not
pleasant, and at the same time, they need not be
disastrous either.

When you find you are in a challenging spot or that
communication is not flowing, a good way to get
through it, and not just around it, is to take whatever
word or issue has come up and hone in on it. Yes,
address it directly…only with a question rather than
an attack or defensive posturing. The language
"XYZ means a lot of different things to different
people, since it seems we are on two different pages
regarding XYZ, please share with me what it means
to you so I can get on the same page with you."

Let's say someone is complaining about service,
and after speaking with that person, you are still at
an impasse, a way to calm the situation and redirect
to a new beginning, you could say, "Good service
means something different to different people, and
we seem to be on two different pages with this, so
please tell me what you were expecting as good
service so we can get on the same page and move
toward a resolution."

The same could be true in a meeting where people are talking about an ad campaign or brand where you were seeking something humorous, yet cannot reach agreement. You could announce, "Humor means something different to different people, and we seem to be on many different pages with this, so please share what you were seeking as humor so we can get on the same page and move toward a decision."

Simply fill in whatever issue/difference you are having in the statement, be sincere in your intent, follow it with focused and open listening, and watch the change in your results!

LUNDBERGism

If you are making *someone* feel uncomfortable, ensure that "someone" is you, and not anybody else!

Chapter 64
The Leadership CAP (Not GAP)

"The purely agitational attitude is not good enough for a detailed consideration of a subject." ~ Jawaharlal Nehru

When caps are not on marker, the marker dries out. Without a cap on one's head in cold weather, the heat escapes. If there is no cap on spending, budgets cannot be met. Similarly, without the Leadership CAP, things get overlooked.

The leadership CAP is a little different, though. Instead of stopping things or shielding things, the leadership CAP allows for growth, and reveals things by having:

Consideration
Appreciation, and
Perspective

for the person/people with whom you are interacting and/or the situation with which you are involved.

Keeping consideration for those involved and the instances, the appreciation for what has been done (or what you expect to be done), and the perspective on what is realistic, you will remain the leader you (and even more so, others) want you to be, and not the micro-manager some become when they are un-**CAP**ped!

Chapter 65
Three R's

"People only see what they are prepared to see." ~ Ralph Waldo Emerson

When many of us were growing up, it was the three R's that were stressed for success. With Reading, wRiting, and aRithmetic as the focus in families, schools, and learning, we knew where we stood with grades and feedback.

In business and life outside school, grades, and feedback are in different formats. For post-school, I encourage you to consider a new approach to the three R's...*Risk, Reward,* and *Repercussion.* With nearly every situation, every opportunity, every challenge, there is *Risk, Reward,* and *Repercussion.* How so? If we assess *Risk*, we know how much we are willing to do or give up to get somewhere.

Assessing *Risk* is what leads to the *Reward* and *Repercussion* portions of our decision-making. Rarely is something a neutral outcome. Sure, we can do nothing, but even doing nothing yields changes likely in the long run. So, along with assessing *Risk*, please review what will be the *Reward* if the *Risk* pays off, and also, what will the *Repercussions* be. It is more fun and engaging to think solely of the outcomes in a positive light, and yet if we are not ready for the possibilities, we too could end up as a statistic of the ill-prepared.

Whether it is something as seemingly small as eating at a new place (*Risk* = not sure about the food/reputation, *Reward* = may find a great place at a good price, *Repercussion* = might not be high quality and may overpay or get sick), or as big as an expansion (*Risk* = not known in the area, *Reward* = grow business, profitability, and reach, *Repercussion* = may be in debt and negatively impact current operations), if you consider the three R's before moving forward, you will be in a solid decision-making mindset to expect the best while being prepared for the worst. And, after all, isn't that the reason we were supposed to focus on Reading, wRiting, and aRithmetic as kids...so we would be in the best position for our future...

LUNDBERGism

It's often not *change* that people dislike or fear; rather it is either *the timing or the way the change was presented or communicated,* that made it uncomfortable for them!

Chapter 66
Happiness…It Is Only Your Responsibility…

"I am only one, but I am one. I cannot do everything, but I can do something. And I will not let what I cannot do interfere with what I can do." ~ Edward Everett Hale

How often have you heard someone say "he makes me happy", or "she's brought happiness to my life"? Worse yet, think back to when someone proclaims, "she just doesn't make me happy," or "he can't seem to make me happy".

These are the words of people who do not comprehend happiness and the opportunity, as well as the responsibility they have for their own happiness.

People neither make us happy or unhappy. Yes, it is true, so true, and yet so surprising to some that I am repeating it here: people neither make us happy or unhappy.

Each of us is responsible for our own happiness, and others either hinder that happiness we have manifested/created, or they enhance it. Those who hinder it are to be kept at arm's length, if not further away from us, and those who enhance it are to be welcomed, and nurtured in a relationship.

This is true for love, friendships, work…everything. If you are thinking "but I have to work with this person, or this person is a family member, and so on", then keep them at a distance, work for your happiness to allow him or her to be who they are with as little impact on you as possible. People do not have to impact you as much as they have, for you are the one who enables each person to have a hold on you or influence over you.

Friendships and relationships are not endurance tests, rather experiences from which to learn and grow. Allowing those who you once thought "did not make you happy" to have an impact on you and your outlook is to give those people some sense of power, and worse yet, relinquish your ability to manage, guide and realize your own happiness.

Remember, if there are people in your life who are not enhancing your happiness, move away from them. This is not to say they are bad people, rather just not good people to interact with you. When the people enhance your happiness, strive to reinforce them and the experiences, feelings, thoughts you have when you are with them by letting them know what you like/appreciate.

Being happy is your role, not that of another person. When you realize or remember that, nobody will have the ability to take it away from you...nobody!

LUNDBERGism

You are responsible for your own happiness! Others simply enhance or hinder it. Keep the enhancers close to you, and the hinderers minimally at arm's-length!

CLOSING COMMENTS

"It is not once nor twice but times without number that the same ideas make their appearance in the world."
~ Aristotle

Thank you for reading this collection of tips and tools for living and learning in an effort to be part of "Reversing the Slobification of America"™! You have been through a Slobification quiz, learned of my approach to four reasons and four drivers, and finished (didn't just 'try' to finish) all three complementary sections on Effective Communication, Professional Behaviors, and Thriving Relationships. Perhaps what you enjoyed most where the "LUNDBERGisms", expressions I use regularly, or the smattering of *Slobification Snippets*, and surely there is no right or wrong answer in where you found value, as it is up to you to do with what you read what you deem fit.

Sure, the drive for creating the three books that lead to this compilation book started when I began to realize years ago that things that I thought were "common sense" (an expression I no longer use) and common courtesies were at best sensible and at worse, quite uncommon to some. Now, with an interest in advancement, growth, and connection, along with a sense of humor about the expression "Reversing the Slobification of America"™, I am thankful for those who buy the book, and grateful to those who read, use, and share the concepts.

I often share one of my first LUNDBERGisms with people after they experience something someone does that was not expected, and that is "People think the way they operate, or the way they have been operated upon. Our challenge as colleagues, friends and leaders is to assess which influence is guiding them and respond accordingly."

Make the assessments and changes one by one. Take the opportunities one at a time. It just takes one – one break, one opportunity, one thing…remember when that one seems like it's never coming that you likely drove a lot of vehicles before buying one, dated a lot of people before you found your soul mate, looked at a lot of places before you settled on where to live…and then you selected one…so you have already proven it just takes one…be that one!

If you are busy reinventing yourself and making changes in your life, keep in mind you have done a lot really well, so also recognize your strengths and successes, and use those as spring-boards for even more to follow! With your school, life and business experience, I trust that the tips and tools here, along with how you operate now, and have been operated upon, will allow you to continue to become what you know and stay on-tract to be a *first-rate you* while you become an ambassador of Effective Communication, Professional Behaviors, and Thriving Relationships in our combined quest to be part of "Reversing the Slobification of America"™!

LUNDBERGism

Under pressure, stress or in uncomfortable situations, we do not do what is right, rather, we do what we know. It will behoove us to practice what we consider to be right so it will eventually become what we know!

Should you want a large quantity of books, or autographed copies of this, or any other books, please email me at Debbie@DebbieLundberg.com.

Feedback on any of my publications is welcomed. I believe *feedback is a gift*, and it is a pleasure to be "present" in people's experiences with my tips!

Finally, if you want to engage me in services, the best way is what is best for you: phone at 813.494.4438, text to the same number, email to Debbie@DebbieLundberg.com, or through my website, www.DebbieLundberg.com.

Thank you, and best wishes on "Reversing the Slobification of America"™!

www.ingramcontent.com/pod-product-compliance
Lightning Source LLC
Chambersburg PA
CBHW031254090426
42742CB00007B/456